Acid Reflux
Diet Cookbook

GERD & LPR-Friendly Recipes for Managing Acid Reflux Symptoms

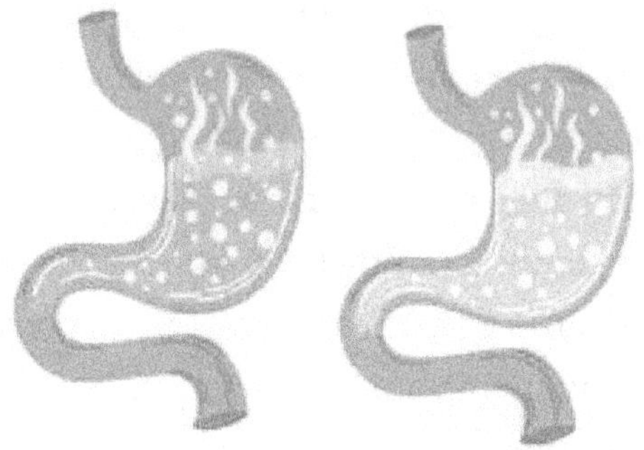

Adam Wood

Copyright © 2023 - All rights reserved.

The content contained within this book may not be reproduced, duplicated, or transmitted without direct written permission from the author or the publisher.

Under no circumstances will any blame or legal responsibility be held against the publisher, or author, for any damages, reparation, or monetary loss due to the information contained within this book. Either directly or indirectly.

Legal Notice: This book is copyright protected. This book is only for personal use. You cannot amend, distribute, sell, use, quote, or paraphrase any part, or the content within this book, without the consent of the author or publisher.

Disclaimer Notice: Please note the information contained within this document is for educational and entertainment purposes only. All effort has been executed to present accurate, up-to-date, and reliable, complete information. No warranties of any kind are declared or implied. Readers acknowledge that the author is not engaging in the rendering of legal, financial, medical, or professional advice. The content within this book has been derived from various sources. Please consult a licensed professional before attempting any techniques outlined in this book.

By reading this document, the reader agrees that under no circumstances is the author responsible for any losses, direct or indirect, which are incurred as a result of the use of the information contained within this document, including, but not limited to, — errors, omissions, or inaccuracies.

Table of Contents

Introduction

Gastric reflux can cause significant discomfort, especially if not properly managed. The good news is that there are plenty of delicious meals that can assist in reducing symptoms and improving overall health. This recipe book is specifically designed for individuals suffering from gastric reflux and is filled with a diverse range of healthy and mouth-watering recipes. The book includes easy-to-follow recipes for breakfast, lunch, dinner, and snacks using common ingredients.

Moreover, you will learn how to modify your eating habits to minimize gastric reflux symptoms. For instance, you will avoid consuming foods that can aggravate symptoms, such as spicy and fatty foods, and instead choose foods that can soothe esophageal irritation, such as leafy green vegetables and rice.

The book will also educate you on what to eat and when to eat to avoid overloading your stomach and triggering reflux. It will help you to avoid consuming large meals at once and to refrain from lying down immediately after eating.

Ultimately, my hope is that this recipe book will enable you to manage your gastric reflux symptoms in an enjoyable and delectable way. I am confident that with this cookbook, you will be able to prepare delicious and healthy meals that will assist you in managing your gastric reflux symptoms and enhancing your quality of life. Bon appétit!

What to Eat

Although there is no one-size-fits-all diet for people with acid reflux, certain foods can help alleviate symptoms and promote overall health. Here is a list of ten foods that are recommended for individuals with acid reflux due to their low acidity and other beneficial properties.

1. Leafy greens: Spinach, kale, and lettuce are low in acid and high in fiber, making them an excellent option for people with acid reflux. They also contribute to neutralizing stomach acid and promoting healthy digestion.

2. Bananas: Bananas are a great choice for people with acid reflux because they are low in acid and high in potassium. Potassium assists in neutralizing stomach acid and can help alleviate acid reflux symptoms.

3. Oatmeal: With its high fiber content and ability to absorb stomach acid, oatmeal is an excellent choice for those suffering from acid reflux. It also improves digestion and can help relieve acid reflux symptoms.

4. Lean proteins: Chicken, fish, and turkey are low in fat and easy to digest, making them helpful in reducing acid reflux symptoms. They also provide the body with essential nutrients that promote overall health.

5. Root vegetables: Potatoes, sweet potatoes, and carrots are low in acid and high in fiber, making them easy to digest and helpful in reducing acid reflux symptoms.

6. Non-citrus fruits: Apples, berries, and melons are low in acid and high in fiber, making them an excellent option for those with acid reflux. They also promote good digestion and can help alleviate acid reflux symptoms.

7. Ginger: Ginger has natural anti-inflammatory properties and can help reduce acid reflux symptoms. It can be taken as tea, a supplement, or mixed with food.

8. Almond milk: Almond milk is a great option for people with acid reflux because it is low in acid and can help neutralize stomach acid. It also improves digestion and helps relieve acid reflux symptoms.

9. Yogurt: Yogurt contains probiotics that help balance the gut microbiota and support good digestion, making it an excellent choice for people with acid reflux.

10. Healthy fats: Avocado, olive oil, and nuts are easy to digest

and can help reduce acid reflux symptoms. They also provide the body with essential nutrients that promote overall health.

What Foods to Avoid

1. Fried and fatty foods: Fried and fatty foods can increase stomach acid production and relax the lower esophageal sphincter, resulting in acid reflux symptoms. Foods such as French fries, fried chicken, and fatty meats should be avoided.
2. Tomato-based products: Tomatoes and tomato-based products are high in acid, which can aggravate acid reflux symptoms. Foods such as pizza, marinara sauce, and salsa should be avoided.
3. Spicy foods: Spicy foods can irritate the esophageal membrane and increase acid production in the stomach, leading to acid reflux symptoms. Hot peppers, curry, and chili should all be avoided.
4. Garlic and onions: Garlic and onions can irritate the esophageal membrane and increase acid production in the stomach, resulting in acid reflux symptoms.
5. Caffeine and other stimulants in chocolate can relax the lower esophageal sphincter, enabling stomach acid to flow back into the esophagus.
6. Peppermint: Peppermint can relax the lower esophageal sphincter, enabling stomach acid to return to the esophagus.
7. It's important to note that some people with acid reflux may have unique food triggers, so it's always a good idea to monitor your own body's reaction to different types of food.

What to Drink

If you have gastroesophageal reflux disease (GERD), it's important to be mindful of what you drink as well as what you eat. Certain beverages can make your symptoms worse, while others can assist to alleviate them. If you have GERD, here are some general tips regarding what to drink and what to avoid:

1. Water: The finest beverage for satisfying thirst and rehydrating your body is water. It's also alkaline, which can improve the neutralization of stomach acid. Drinking water can also be useful to wash out any acid that has refluxed into the esophagus, which can alleviate symptoms. Drink at least 8 glasses of water per day.

2. Low-fat milk or non-dairy alternatives: These can provide a source of calcium and other nutrients, but choose low-fat options to avoid aggravating GERD symptoms. Milk can also help to neutralize stomach acid, providing relief. Non-dairy alternatives such as almond or soy milk are also good options, but be sure to avoid those that are sweetened or flavored.

3. Herbal tea: Some herbal teas, such as ginger, chamomile, or licorice, may help to soothe the digestive system and reduce inflammation. Ginger in particular has been found to have anti-inflammatory properties and can help to reduce the symptoms of GERD.

4. Decaffeinated coffee or tea: Caffeine can aggravate GERD symptoms, so it's best to avoid it. However, some people can tolerate decaffeinated coffee or tea without experiencing symptoms. It's important to monitor your own personal tolerance.

What Drinks to Avoid

1. Alcohol relaxes the lower esophageal sphincter, allowing stomach acid to return to the esophagus. It can also cause an increase in symptoms by stimulating acid production in the stomach. To reduce GERD symptoms, restrict or limit your alcohol consumption.

2. Carbonated drinks: The bubbles in carbonated drinks can cause stomach distention, which can trigger reflux. Carbonated beverages can also increase acid production in the stomach, causing symptoms to worsen.

3. Citrus juices: These can be high in acid and can irritate the

esophagus. The acidity in citrus juices can also stimulate acid production in the stomach, leading to increased symptoms.

4. Coffee and tea with caffeine: As mentioned earlier, caffeine can aggravate GERD symptoms. It's best to avoid it, or limit your intake to minimize symptoms.

Best Tips and Tricks to Avoid Gastric Reflux

1. Avoid spicy, greasy, and fatty foods: These types of foods can increase acid production in the stomach and worsen acid reflux symptoms. The lower esophageal sphincter may also relax as a result, enabling stomach acid to flow back into the esophagus.
2. Eat small, frequent meals instead of large meals: Eating smaller, more frequent meals can help reduce the amount of acid in the stomach and prevent acid reflux. Large meals can lead the stomach to create more acid, which can then reflux into the esophagus.
3. Avoid eating close to bedtime: Eating close to bedtime can cause acid reflux symptoms to worsen as gravity is not helping keep stomach contents where they should be. When we lie down, it makes it easier for stomach acid to flow back into the esophagus, so it's best to avoid eating for at least 2-3 hours before going to bed.
4. Elevate the head of your bed: Elevating the head of your bed can help reduce nighttime acid reflux by allowing gravity to keep stomach contents where they should be. This can be accomplished by placing blocks below the bed's foot or by utilizing a foam wedge pillow.
5. Try to maintain a healthy weight: Being overweight can increase the risk of acid reflux, so try to maintain a healthy weight to reduce symptoms. Extra weight puts strain on the stomach, causing acid to run back into the esophagus.
6. Cook with low-acid ingredients such as vegetables and lean proteins: Cooking with lowacid ingredients can help reduce

acid reflux symptoms as they are less likely to aggravate the condition. Some examples of low-acid foods include leafy greens, broccoli, asparagus, lean meats, fish, and poultry.

7. Avoid alcohol and caffeine: Both can relax the lower esophageal sphincter, allowing stomach acid to flow back into the esophagus. They also increase stomach acid production, which can aggravate acid reflux symptoms.

8. Chew your food thoroughly: Chewing your food thoroughly can help to reduce the amount of acid needed to digest it. This can help prevent acid reflux symptoms from occurring.

9. Watch your medications: Certain medications such as anti-inflammatory drugs, calcium channel blockers, and antidepressants can relax the lower esophageal sphincter and increase the risk of acid reflux. If you are using any of these medications, please check with your doctor about possible alternatives.

10. Use stress-relief techniques: Stress can increase stomach acid production and relax the lower esophageal sphincter, both of which can cause acid reflux symptoms. Try relaxation techniques like yoga or meditation to relieve tension.

Breakfasts

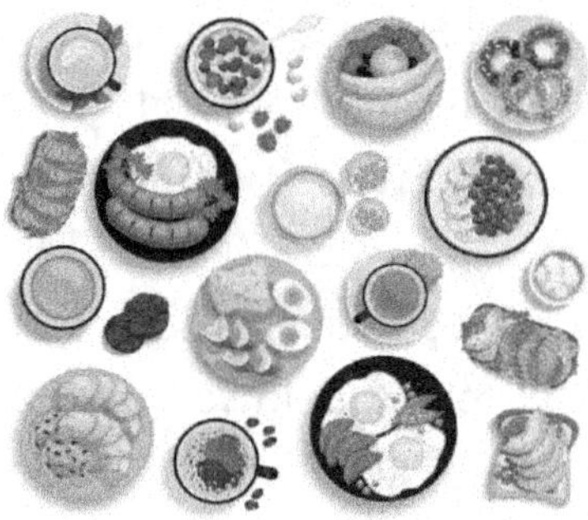

Low Fat Greek Yogurt with Acai Berry Granola

Preparation Time: 5 minutes | Cooking Time: 5 minutes

Servings: 2

Ingredients:

- 2 cups nonfat Greek yogurt
- 2 tsp raw honey
- 1/2 cup granola cereal
- 1/2 cup acai berries, frozen

Directions:

1. Pour the yogurt into a serving bowl or a glass and stir in raw honey and top with granola, sprinkle acai berries on top. Enjoy!

Nutrition:

Calories: 230 kcal; Total Fat: 18.2 g; Total Carbohydrates: 45.5 g; Protein: 29.1 g

Ginger and Turmeric Detox Tea

Preparation Time: 10 minutes | Cooking Time: 20 minutes

Servings: 2

Ingredients:

- 6 bags green tea
- 2 cups water
- 1 cup fresh ginger, chopped
- 3 cinnamon sticks
- 1 tsp turmeric, ground

Directions:

1. Add chopped ginger and green tea bags to a pan of water and bring to a rolling boil.
2. Lower heat and simmer for about 10 minutes.
3. Add in turmeric, and cinnamon stick, and cook for another 10 minutes. remove the pan from heat and let cool before straining.
4. Refrigerate for at least 1 hour or until chilled.

Nutrition:

Calories: 194 kcal; Total Fat: 3.9 g; Total Carbohydrates: 37.1 g; Protein: 4.2 g

★ ★ ★ ★ ★

Active Weight Loss Tea

Preparation Time: 10 minutes | Cooking Time: 1 hour 20 minutes

Servings: 2

Ingredients:

- 4 cups hot water
- 1-inch ginger root, thinly sliced
- 2 cinnamon sticks
- 4 green tea bags

Directions:

1. Add the hot water to a large pot over high heat and add the cinnamon stick and sliced ginger. Bring to a boil then turn off the heat. Add the tea bags and let the tea steep.
2. You can drink this tea as is or sweeten it with some raw honey.
3. Sip on this tea first thing in the morning, before your breakfast, and the last thing before you sleep for maximum fat-burning benefits.

Nutrition:

Calories: 47 kcal; Total Fat: 1.2 g; Total Carbohydrates: 7.5 g; Protein: 1.3 g

★ ★ ★ ★ ★

Fruity Detox Tea

Preparation Time: 10 minutes | Cooking Time: 1 hour 20 minutes

Servings: 1

Ingredients:

- 2 cucumber slices
- 2 strawberries, thinly sliced
- 1 green tea bag
- 1 tsp raw honey
- 1 cup boiling water

Directions:

1. Add the tea bag to the cup of water and let steep until it cools completely. Stir in all the remaining ingredients and you are ready to drink.
2. You can add some ice cubes if you like your tea super chilled.

Nutrition:

Calories: 49 kcal; Total Fat: 0.2 g; Total Carbohydrates: 12 g; Protein: 0.9 g

Superfood Overnight Oats

Preparation Time: 10 minutes | Cooking Time: 0 minutes

Servings: 2

Ingredients:

- 1/2 cup old-fashioned oats
- 1 tsp chia seeds
- 1/2 cup vanilla almond milk, unsweetened
- 1/4 cup fresh blueberries
- 1/4 banana, chopped
- 1/4 cup fresh pineapple, chopped
- 1/4 cup nonfat Greek yogurt
- 1/4 tsp cinnamon

Directions:

1. In a small jar, combine oats, chia seeds, almond milk, blueberries, banana, pineapple, yogurt, and cinnamon. Refrigerate overnight.
2. To serve, remove from the fridge and stir to mix well before serving.

Nutrition:

Calories: 310 kcal; Total Fat: 8.4 g; Total Carbohydrates: 29 g; Protein: 10.8 g

★ ★ ★ ★ ★

Ginger Almond Berry Smoothie Bowl

Preparation Time: 10 minutes | Cooking Time: 0 minutes

Servings: 2

Ingredients:

- 1 cup unsweetened almond milk

- 1 scoop vanilla protein powder
- 1 tbsp flaxseed, ground
- 1 cup kale, chopped
- 1 tsp fresh ginger, minced
- 1 cup spinach, frozen, chopped
- 1 cup blueberries
- 1 cup strawberries

Directions:

1. Combine all ingredients in a blender and blend until very smooth and creamy. Divide the smoothie between serving bowls and top each with your favorite toppings. Enjoy!

Nutrition:

Calories: 222 kcal; Total Fat: 8.2 g; Total Carbohydrates: 8.1 g; Protein: 3.7 g

Citrus Turmeric Smoothie

Preparation Time: 5 minutes | Cooking Time: 5 minutes

Servings: 2

Ingredients:

- 1 tsp turmeric
- 1/2 orange, segmented
- 1 cup Greek yogurt
- 1/2 cup mango chunks
- 1/2 cup almond milk
- 1 banana, sliced

Directions:

1. Blend all ingredients until very smooth. Enjoy!

Nutrition:

Calories: 209 kcal; Total Fat: 3.8 g; Total Carbohydrates: 32.8 g; Protein: 13.6 g

★ ★ ★ ★ ★

Chai Spiced Greek Yogurt Parfait with Fresh Fruits

Preparation Time: 10 minutes |Cooking Time: 0 minutes Servings: 4 Ingredients:

- 1 cup granola cereal
- 2 cups non-fat Greek yogurt
- 1/2 tsp allspice, ground
- 1/2 tsp ginger, ground
- 1/2 tsp cardamom, ground
- 1/2 tsp cloves, ground
- 1/2 tsp nutmeg, ground
- 1/2 tsp cinnamon, ground
- 1 banana, sliced
- 1 cup apricots, halved

Directions:

1. In a small bowl, stir together yogurt and spices until well combined.
2. Sprinkle a small layer of granola in a serving glass and then top with a layer of yogurt mixture followed by banana slices and apricot halves; repeat the layers to fill the glasses.
3. Enjoy!

Nutrition:

Calories: 207 kcal; Total Fat: 8.4 g; Total Carbohydrates: 48.6 g; Protein: 20.2 g

★ ★ ★ ★ ★

Wholesome Buckwheat Pancakes

Preparation Time: 10 minutes | Cooking Time: 10 minutes

Servings: 2

Ingredients:

- 2/3 cup raw buckwheat groats, soaked overnight, and rinsed
- 1 egg
- 1/4 tsp cinnamon
- 1 tsp stevia
- 1/4 tsp sea salt
- 1/2 cup water

Directions:

1. Transfer rinsed and drained buckwheat to a blender and add in egg, stevia, cinnamon, salt, and water and blend until very smooth.
2. Grease a nonstick skillet and set over medium heat; pour in about a third cup of the buckwheat batter, spreading to cover the bottom of the skillet.
3. Cook for about 2 minutes over the side until the pancake is golden brown. Repeat with the remaining batter.
4. Serve right away with a glass of orange juice.

Nutrition:

Calories: 166 kcal; Total Fat: 3.5 g; Total Carbohydrates: 26.4 g; Protein: 7.8 g

★ ★ ★ ★ ★

Oats with Berries

Preparation time: 10 minutes | Cooking time: 30 minutes

Servings: 4

Ingredients:

- 1 cup Steel Cut Oats
- Dash of Salt
- 3 cups Water

For toppings:

- 1/2 cup Berries of your choice
- 1/4 cup Nuts or Seeds of your choice like Almonds or Hemp Seeds

Directions:

1. To begin with, place the oats in a small saucepan and heat it over medium-high heat.
2. Now, toast it for 3 minutes while stirring the pan frequently.
3. Next, pour water to the saucepan and mix well.
4. Allow the mixture to boil. Lower the heat.
5. Allow it to cook for 23 to 25 minutes or until the oats are cooked and tender.
6. Once done cooking, transfer the mixture to the serving bowl and top it with the berries and seeds.
7. Serve it warm or cold.
8. Tip: If you desire, you can add sweeteners like maple syrup or coconut sugar or stevia to it.

Nutrition:

Calories: 118Kcal; Protein: 4.1g; Carbohydrates: 16.5g; Fat: 4.4g;

★ ★ ★ ★ ★

Golden Beet and Spinach Frittata

Preparation Time: 15 minutes or fewer | Cooking Time: 5 to 7 hours on low | Servings: 4–6

Ingredients:

- 1 tbsp extra-virgin olive oil
- 8 large eggs
- 1 cup packed fresh spinach leaves, chopped
- 1 cup golden beets, diced and peeled
- 1/4 cup unsweetened almond milk
- 3/4 tsp sea salt
- 1/2 tsp basil leaves, dried
- Black pepper, freshly ground

Directions:

1. Coat the slow cooker with olive oil.
2. In a large bowl, combine the eggs, spinach, beets, almond milk, salt, and basil, and season with pepper. Whisk together and pour the custard into the slow cooker.
3. Cover the cooker and set it to low. Cook for 5 to 7 hours, or until the eggs are completely set, and serve.

Storage tip:

This frittata should keep in the refrigerator for up to 3 days. Keep in mind that overheating the frittata to warm it could cause the eggs to become rubbery.

Nutrition:

Calories: 202 kcal; Total Fat: 14 g; Total Carbohydrates: 6 g; Sugar: 4 g

Spinach Avocado Smoothie

Preparation time: 5 minutes | Cooking time: 5 minutes

Servings: 1

Ingredients:

- 1/4 of 1 Avocado
- 1 cup Plain Yoghurt, non-Fat
- 2 tbsp. Water
- 1 cup Spinach, fresh
- 1 tsp. Honey
- 1 Banana, frozen

Directions:

1. Start by blending all the ingredients needed to make the smoothie in a high-speed blender for 2 to 3 minutes or until you get a smooth and creamy mixture.
2. Next, transfer the mixture to a serving glass.
3. Serve and enjoy.

Tip:

If you don't prefer to use yogurt, you can use unsweetened almond milk.

Nutrition:

Calories: 357Kcal; Protein: 7.7g; Carbohydrates: 37.8g; Fat: 8.2g

★ ★ ★ ★ ★

Golden Milk

Preparation time: 5 minutes | Cooking time: 5 minutes

Servings: 2

Ingredients:

- 1 tbsp. Coconut Oil
- 1 1/2 cups Coconut Milk, light
- Pinch of Pepper
- 1 1/2 cups Almond Milk, unsweetened
- 1/4 tsp. Ginger, grated
- 1 1/2 tsp. Turmeric, grounded
- 1/4 tsp. Cinnamon, grounded
- Sweetener of your choice, as needed

Directions:

1. To make this healthy beverage, you need to place all the ingredients in a medium-sized saucepan and mix it well.
2. After that, heat it over medium heat for 3 to 4 minutes or until it is hot but not boiling. Stir continuously.
3. Taste for seasoning. Add more sweetener or spice as required by you.
4. Finally, transfer the milk to the serving glass and enjoy it.

Tip:

Instead of cinnamon powder, you can also use the cinnamon stick, which can be discarded at the end if you prefer a much more intense flavor.

Nutrition:

Calories: 205Kcal; Protein: 3.2g; Carbohydrates: 8.9g; Fat: 19.5g

★ ★ ★ ★ ★

Overnight Coconut Chia Oats

Preparation time: 10 minutes | Cooking time: 60 minutes

Servings: 1 to 2

Ingredients:

- 1/2 cup Coconut Milk, unsweetened
- 2 tsp. Chia Seeds
- 1 1/2 cups Old Fashioned Oats, whole grain
- 1/2 tsp. Cinnamon, grounded
- 1 cup Almond Milk, unsweetened
- 1/2 tsp. Cinnamon, grounded
- 2 tsp. Date Syrup
- 1/2 tsp. Black Pepper, grounded
- 1 tsp. Turmeric, grounded

Directions:

1. To start with, keep the oats in the mason jar.
2. After that, mix the rest of the ingredients in a medium bowl until combined well.
3. Then, pour the mixture to the jars and stir well.
4. Now, close the jar and place it in the refrigerator overnight.
5. In the morning, stir the mixture and then enjoy it.

Tip:

You can top it with toasted nuts or berries.

Nutrition:

Calories: 335Kcal; Protein: 8g; Carbohydrates: 34.1g; Fat: 19.9g

★ ★ ★ ★ ★

Blueberry Hemp Seed Smoothie

Preparation time: 10 minutes | Cooking time: 5 minutes

Servings: 1

Ingredients:

- 1 1/4 cup Blueberries, frozen
- 1 1/4 cup Plant-Based Milk of your choice
- 2 tbsp. Hemp Seeds
- 1 tsp. Spirulina
- 1 scoop of Protein: Powder

Directions:

1. First, place all the ingredients needed to make the smoothie in a high-speed blender and blend them for 2 minutes or until smooth.
2. Transfer the mixture to a serving glass and enjoy it.

Tip:

Instead of blueberries, you can use any berries of your choice.

Nutrition:

Calories: 493Kcal; Protein: 37.8g; Carbohydrates: 46.3g; Fat: 19.6g

★ ★ ★ ★ ★

Chia Pudding with Oats, Strawberries, and Kiwi

Preparation time: 25 minutes | Cooking time: 0 minutes

Servings: 2

Ingredients:

- 2 cups unsweetened almond milk

- 1 cup chia seeds
- 1/4 cup maple syrup
- 1/2 teaspoon vanilla extract
- 1/2 cup toasted oats
- 4 large strawberries, sliced
- 1 kiwi, peeled and sliced

Directions:

1. In a quart-size jar with a tight-fitting lid, combine the milk, chia seeds, maple syrup, and vanilla. Cover and shake well, then set aside for at least 15 minutes for the pudding to thicken. (This can even be done the night before and refrigerated overnight.)

2. Divide the pudding between two serving dishes, top with the toasted oats, strawberries, and kiwi, and serve.

Nutrition:

Calories: 360Kcal; Protein: 8g; Carbohydrates: 60g; Fat: 11g

★ ★ ★ ★ ★

Roasted Almonds

Preparation time: 5 minutes | Cooking time: 10 minutes

Servings: 20

Ingredients:

- 2 cups whole almonds
- 1/2 teaspoon ground cinnamon
- 1/2 teaspoon ground cumin
- 1/2 teaspoon ground coriander
- Salt and freshly ground black pepper, to taste
- 1 tablespoon extra-virgin organic olive oil

Directions:

1. Preheat the oven to 350 deg. F. Line a baking dish with a

parchment paper.

2. In a bowl, add all ingredients and toss to coat well.

3. Transfer the almond mixture into prepared baking dish in a single layer.

4. Roast for around 10 minutes, flipping twice inside the middle way.

5. Remove from oven and make aside to cool down the completely before serving.

6. You can preserve these roasted almonds in airtight jar.

Nutrition:

Calories: 62Kcal; Protein: 5g; Carbohydrates: 12g; Fat: 7g

Roasted Pumpkin Seeds

Preparation time: 10 minutes | Cooking time: 20 minutes

Servings: 4

Ingredients:

- 1 cup pumpkin seeds, washed and dried
- 2 teaspoons garam masala
- 1/4 teaspoon ground turmeric
- Salt, to taste
- 3 tablespoons coconut oil, meted

Directions:

1. Preheat the oven to 350 deg. F.
2. In a bowl, add all ingredients and toss to coat well.
3. Transfer the almond mixture right into a baking sheet.
4. Roast approximately twenty or so minutes, flipping occasionally.
5. Remove from oven and make aside to cool completely before serving.

Nutrition:

Calories: 136Kcal; Protein: 12g; Carbohydrates: 9g; Fat: 14g

Egg Cups

Preparation Time: 45 minutes | Cooking Time: 12 minutes

Portions: 6

Ingredients:

- 3 C. shiitake mushrooms
- 2 leaves kale
- 1 tsp. turmeric
- 1/2 tsp. dried thyme
- 1/2 tsp. oregano
- 1 tsp. salt
- 1 tsp. freshly ground pepper
- 1 tsp. olive oil
- 10 eggs
- 1/2 C. yeast

Direction:

1. Finely chop mushrooms, and kale. Sauté oregano, turmeric, thyme, salt, and pepper and olive oil over a medium heat until spices are fragrant.
2. Add the mushrooms and kale, and continue cooking, stirring frequently, until the kale is bright green. Distribute mushroom mixture to ten muffin tins. Crack an egg into each tin.
3. Bake for twelve minutes at 400°F. Allow it to set for a few minutes before serving. Enjoy.

Nutrition:

Calories: 289 Fat: 9 g Protein: 21 g Carbohydrates: 9 g.

Vegetarians Mains

Apples Mix

Preparation time: 10 minutes | Cooking time: 7 hours

Servings: 10

INGREDIENTS:

- 2 green apples, cored and cut into wedges
- 3 pounds sweet potatoes, peeled and cut into medium wedges
- 1 cup almond milk
- 1 cup apple butter
- 1 and 1/2 teaspoon pumpkin pie spice

DIRECTIONS:

1. In your slow cooker, mix sweet potatoes with green apples, milk, apple butter, and spice, toss, cover, and cook on Low for 7 hours.
2. Toss, divide between plates, and serve as a side dish.

NUTRITION:

288 calories, 2.9g protein, 57.4g carbohydrates, 6.1g fat, 7.6g fiber, 0mg cholesterol, 20mg sodium, 1247mg potassium.

Asparagus Mix

Preparation time: 10 minutes | Cooking time: 5 hours

Servings: 4

INGREDIENTS:

- 2 pounds asparagus spears, cut into medium pieces
- 1 cup mushrooms, sliced
- A drizzle of olive oil
- 1 cups of coconut milk

- 5 eggs, whisked

DIRECTIONS:

1. Grease your Slow cooker with the oil and spread asparagus and mushrooms on the bottom.
2. In a bowl, mix the eggs with milk, and whisk, pour into the slow cooker, toss everything, cover and cook on Low for 6 hours.
3. Divide between plates and serve as a side dish.

NUTRITION:

404 calories,15.2g protein, 65.5g carbohydrates, 34.4g fat, 7.6g fiber, 205mg cholesterol, 101mg sodium, 903mg potassium.

Asparagus and Eggs Mix

Preparation time: 10 minutes | Cooking time: 6 hours

Servings: 4

INGREDIENTS:

- 10 ounces cream of celery
- 12 ounces asparagus, chopped
- 2 eggs, hard-boiled, peeled, and sliced
- 5 oz. tofu, crumbled
- 1 teaspoon olive oil

DIRECTIONS:

1. Grease your Slow cooker with the oil, add cream of celery and tofu to the slow cooker and stir.
2. Add asparagus and eggs, cover, and cook on Low for 6 hours.
3. Divide between plates and serve as a side dish.

NUTRITION:

134 calories,8.5g protein, 9.1g carbohydrates, 8.1g fat, 2.5g fiber,

90mg cholesterol, 573mg sodium, 323mg potassium.

Okra and Mushrooms Side Dish

Preparation time: 10 minutes | Cooking time: 3 hours

Servings: 4

INGREDIENTS:

- 2 cups okra, sliced
- 3 1/2 cups zucchini, sliced
- 1 cup white mushrooms, sliced
- 1/2 cup olive oil
- 1/2 cup balsamic vinegar
- 2 tablespoons basil, chopped
- 1 tablespoon thyme, chopped

DIRECTIONS:

1. In your slow cooker, mix okra with zucchini, mushrooms, basil, and thyme.
2. In bowl mix oil with vinegar, whisk well, add to the slow cooker, cover and cook on High for 3 hours.

NUTRITION:

304 calories,5.9g protein, 17.7g carbohydrates, 15.8g fat, 5.1g fiber, 0mg cholesterol, 19mg sodium, 703mg potassium.

Okra and Corn Bowls

Preparation time: 10 minutes | Cooking time: 8 hours

Servings: 4

INGREDIENTS:

- 1 cup of water
- 16 ounces okra, sliced
- 2 cups corn kernels
- 1 and 1/2 teaspoon smoked paprika
- 28 ounces canned zucchini, crushed
- 1 teaspoon oregano, dried
- 1 teaspoon thyme, dried
- 1 teaspoon marjoram, dried

DIRECTIONS:

1. In your slow cooker, mix water, okra, corn, paprika, zucchini, oregano, thyme, marjoram, and cover, cook on Low for 8 hours, divide between plates and serve as a side dish.

NUTRITION:

171 calories, 2.3g protein, 36.2g carbohydrates, 1.8g fat, 9.6g fiber, 0mg cholesterol, 33mg sodium, 1138mg potassium.

★ ★ ★ ★ ★

Roasted Beets with Olive Oil

Preparation time: 10 minutes | Cooking time: 4 hours

Servings: 5

INGREDIENTS:

- 10 small beets
- 3 teaspoons olive oil

DIRECTIONS:

2. Divide each beet on a tin foil piece, drizzle oil, wrap beets in the foil, place them in your slow cooker, cover and cook on High for 4 hours.

3. Unwrap beets, cool them down a bit, peel, and slice and serve them as a side dish.

NUTRITION:

128 calories,3.4g protein, 19.9g carbohydrates, 5g fat, 4g fiber, 0mg cholesterol, 154mg sodium, 610mg potassium.

Beets with White Vinegar

Preparation time: 10 minutes | Cooking time: 8 hours

Servings: 6

INGREDIENTS:

- 6 beets, peeled and cut into medium wedges
- 2 tablespoons honey
- 2 tablespoons olive oil
- 1 tablespoon white vinegar

DIRECTIONS:

1. In your Slow cooker, mix beets with honey, oil, vinegar, cover, and cook on Low for 8 hours.

2. Divide between plates and serve as a side dish.

NUTRITION:

107 calories,1.7g protein, 15.9g carbohydrates, 4.9g fat, 2g fiber, 0mg cholesterol, 78mg sodium, 317mg potassium.

Summer Mix

Preparation time: 10 minutes

Cooking time: 2 hours Servings: 4

INGREDIENTS:

- 1/4 cup olive oil
- 2 tablespoons basil, chopped
- 2 tablespoons balsamic vinegar
- 2 teaspoons mustard
- 3 summer squash, sliced
- 2 zucchinis, sliced

DIRECTIONS:

1. In your Slow cooker, mix squash with zucchinis, mustard, vinegar, basil, and oil, toss a bit, cover, and cook on High for 2 hours.
2. Divide between plates and serve as a side dish.

NUTRITION:

154 calories,2.7g protein, 8.2g carbohydrates, 13.5g fat, 2.4g fiber, 0mg cholesterol, 13mg sodium, 495mg potassium.

Tarragon Beets

Preparation time: 10 minutes | Cooking time: 7 hours

Servings: 4

INGREDIENTS:

- 6 medium assorted-color beets, peeled and cut into wedges
- 2 tablespoons balsamic vinegar
- 2 tablespoons olive oil
- 2 tablespoons chives, chopped

- 1 tablespoon tarragon, chopped
- 1 teaspoon orange peel, grated

DIRECTIONS:

1. In your Slow cooker, mix beets with vinegar, oil, chives, tarragon, and orange peel, cover, and cook on Low for 7 hours.
2. Divide between plates and serve as a side dish.

NUTRITION: 130 calories,2.7g protein, 15.4g carbohydrates, 7.3g fat, 3.1g fiber, 0mg cholesterol, 116mg sodium, 482mg potassium.

Instant Pot Braised Kale and Carrots

Preparation Time: 5 minutes | Cooking Time: 12 minutes

Servings: 6

INGREDIENTS

- 1 tablespoon olive oil
- 1 carrot, peeled and julienned
- 3 cups of kale, chopped
- 1/2 cup water
- Salt to taste

DIRECTIONS:

1. Press the Sauté button on the Instant Pot and heat the oil.
2. Add the rest of the ingredients.
3. Close the lid and make sure that the steam release valve is set to "Sealing."
4. Press the Manual button and adjust the cooking time to 10 minutes.
5. Do quick pressure release.

NUTRITION:

Calories per serving: 107; Carbohydrates: 8.5g; Protein: 1.4g; Fat:

2.4g; Sugar: 0g; Sodium: 14mg; Fiber: 5.3g

★ ★ ★ ★ ★

Buckwheat Tabbouleh

Preparation Time: 15 minutes | Cooking Time: 10 minutes

Servings: 4

Ingredients:
- 1 tbsp olive oil
- 2 cups buckwheat, cooked
- 1/4 cup fresh mint, chopped
- 1/2 cup fresh parsley, chopped
- Sea salt

Directions:

1. Heat the olive oil in your large skillet over medium-high heat.
2. Add the buckwheat. Sauté until heated through, about 5 minutes.
3. Add the mint and parsley, stir well and sauté for another 1 minute.
4. Remove from the heat and with sea salt to season.

Nutrition:

Calories: 184 kcal; Protein: 6 g; Carbohydrates: 34 g; Fat: 5 g

★ ★ ★ ★ ★

Instant Pot Miso Soup with Shitake and Bok Choy

Preparation Time: 5 minutes | Cooking Time: 10 minutes

Servings: 3

INGREDIENTS

- 1 teaspoon red miso paste

- 2 1/2 cups water
- 2 teaspoons soy sauce
- 2 thin slices of ginger
- 3 large shitake mushrooms, sliced
- 1 small head baby bok choy, sliced

DIRECTIONS:

1. Place all ingredients in the Instant Pot.
2. Give a good stir.
3. Close the lid and make sure that the steam release valve is set to "Sealing."
4. Press the Soup button and adjust the cooking time to 10 minutes.
5. Do quick pressure release.

NUTRITION:

Calories per serving:56; Carbohydrates: 9.9g; Protein: 3.5g; Fat: 1.1g; Sugar: 0g; Sodium: 155mg; Fiber: 6.3g

Sweet Life Bowl

Preparation Time: 15 minutes | Cooking Time: 5 minutes

Servings: 2

Ingredients:

- 2 baby spinach
- 1 cup zucchini, sliced in half
- 4 carrots, peeled and thinly sliced
- 3 stalks celery, thinly sliced
- 2 tbsp olive oil or coconut oil
- 2 cups brown rice /quinoa, cooked
- 1 cup chickpeas, cooked, rinsed, and drained

- 1/4 cup pecans, toasted, chopped
- 1 bunch kale
- 1/2 cup fresh parsley
- Fresh pepper and sea salt, for taste

For the dressing:

- 2 tbsp olive oil
- 1 tsp Dijon mustard
- 1 tsp maple syrup or raw honey
- 1/4 tsp red pepper flakes
- 1/2 inch fresh ginger

Directions:

1. Start by reheating the brown rice or quinoa and share into 2 different bowls. Get a large pan and heat over medium-high heat and add coconut or olive oil.
2. Stir in carrots, and celery. Sauté veggies for 3–4 minutes until they become soft and turn brownish. In the fourth minute, add chickpeas and roasted cauliflower.
3. Add sliced kale and allow it to wilt for about a minute. Take off the pan from heat. Add zucchini and baby spinach and stir so that the vegetable heat cooks the zucchini and spinach.
4. Now, pour the sautéed mix over the quinoa and brown rice. Sprinkle pepper and sea salt and supplement it with dried fruit.

Making Turmeric Roasted Cauliflower:

1. Preheat the oven to 400°F. Get a roasting pan and oil lightly. Get a mixing bowl, and add cauliflower alongside turmeric, pepper, salt, and olive oil.
2. Set the bowl on the roasting pan and roast for 20–25 minutes until the edges change to a golden brown.

Making the dressing:

1. In a mixing bowl, mix the mustard, honey, red pepper flakes, and ginger.

2. Gently whisk in the olive oil, the idea is to form an emulsion.

3. Sprinkle the dressing over the bowls.

4. Toss gently. The toppings should be fresh parsley and toasted pecans.

Nutrition:

Calories: 158 kcal; Protein: 18 g; Carbohydrates: 20 g; Fat: 16 g

★ ★ ★ ★ ★

Coriander and Mint With Turmeric Roasted Cauliflower

Preparation Time: 15 minutes | Cooking Time: 15 minutes

Servings: 4

Ingredients:

- 1 tbsp cumin, ground
- 1/4 cup pine nuts
- 2 tsp turmeric, ground
- 2 tbsp coconut oil
- 2 tbsp cilantro/coriander, roughly chopped
- 1 tbsp mint, chopped roughly
- 1 large cauliflower, broken down into bite-sized florets
- Himalayan salt to taste

Directions:

1. Preheat the oven to 220°C. Get a clean, large bowl and combine the turmeric, coconut oil, and ½ tsp salt with your hands. Add the cauliflower florets and mix them in properly.

2. Take off the cauliflower and spread it on a big baking tray. Slot the tray straight into the preheated oven for between 15–20 minutes until it softens and turns brown. Get a smaller baking trail, pour the pine on it and place it in the oven for

about a minute.

3. Lastly, move the cauliflower to a serving bowl, and sprinkle some pine nuts, mint, and cilantro/coriander. Then serve.

Nutrition:

Calories: 150 kcal; Protein: 21 g; Carbohydrates: 19 g; Fat: 10 g

★ ★ ★ ★ ★

Asparagus Cheese Vermicelli

Preparation Time: 10 minutes | Cooking Time: 15 minutes

Servings: 4

Ingredients:

- 2 tsp olive oil, divided
- 6 asparagus spears, cut into pieces
- 4 oz. whole-grain vermicelli, dried
- 1 medium zucchini, chopped
- 2 tbsp fresh basil, chopped
- 4 tbsp Parmesan, freshly grated, divided
- 1/8 tsp black pepper, ground

Directions:

1. Add 1 tsp oil to a skillet and heat it. Stir in asparagus and sauté until golden brown.
2. Cut the sautéed asparagus into 1-inch pieces. Fill a sauce pot with water up to 3/4 full. After boiling the water, add pasta and cook for 10 minutes until it is all done.
3. Drain and rinse the pasta under tap water. Add pasta to a large bowl, then toss in olive oil, zucchini, asparagus, basil, and parmesan. Serve with black pepper on top.

Nutrition:

Calories: 325 kcal; Protein: 7.3 g; Carbohydrates: 48 g; Fat: 8 g

* * * * *

Sweet Potato

Preparation Time:20 minutes | Cooking Time:20 minutes

Servings:6

Ingredients:

- 2 tsp olive oil
- 1 tbsp fresh ginger, grated and peeled
- 2 cups sweet potatoes, diced and peeled
- 1 cup carrots, diced
- 1 cup water
- 1/2 cup heavy (whipping) cream
- 1 tsp cumin, ground
- 2 tbsp low-fat plain yogurt
- 2 tbsp fresh cilantro, chopped

Directions:

1. In a large saucepan overheat, heat the olive oil.
2. Add the ginger and sauté until softened, about 3 minutes.
3. Add the sweet potatoes, carrots, water, cream, and cumin and stir to mix well. Bring the mixture to a boil. Lessen the heat to low, and simmer until the vegetables are tender, about 15 minutes.
4. Serve immediately, topped with yogurt and cilantro.

Nutrition:

Calories: 132 kcal; Protein: 6 g; Carbohydrates: 16 g; Fat: 9 g

* * * * *

Zucchini Noodles with Spring Vegetables

Preparation Time: 20 minutes | Cooking Time: 10 minutes

Servings: 6

Ingredients:

- 6 zucchinis, cut into long noodles
- 1 cup snow peas, halved
- 1 cup (3-inch pieces) of asparagus
- 1 tbsp olive oil
- 1 cup fresh spinach, shredded
- 3/4 cup zucchini, halved
- 2 tbsp fresh basil leaves, chopped

Directions:

1. Fill a medium pan with water, place over medium-high heat, and bring to a boil.
2. Reduce the heat to medium, and blanch the zucchini ribbons, snow peas, and asparagus by submerging them in the water for 1 minute. Drain and rinse immediately under cold water. **3.** Pat the vegetables dry with paper towels and transfer them to a large bowl.
3. Place an average skillet over medium heat, and increase the olive oil. Sauté until tender, about 3 minutes.
4. Add the spinach, and sauté until the spinach is wilted, about 3 minutes.
5. Add the zucchini mixture, the zucchini, and basil, and toss until well combined.
6. Serve immediately.

Nutrition:

Calories: 52 kcal; Protein: 2 g; Carbohydrates: 4 g; Fat: 2 g

★ ★ ★ ★ ★

Butternut-Squash Macaroni and Cheese

Preparation Time: 15 minutes | Cooking Time: 20 minutes

Servings: 2

Ingredients:

- 1 cup whole-wheat ziti macaroni
- 2 cups butternut squash, peeled and cubed
- 1 cup non-fat or low-Fat milk, divided
- Black pepper, freshly ground
- 1 tsp Dijon mustard
- 1 tbsp olive oil
- 1/4 cup low-fat cheese, shredded

Directions:

1. Cook the pasta al dente. Put the butternut squash plus ½ cup milk in a medium saucepan and place over medium-high heat. Season with black pepper. Bring it to a simmer. Lower the heat, then cook until fork-tender, 8 to 10 minutes.
2. In a blender, add squash and Dijon mustard. Purée until smooth. In the meantime, place a huge sauté pan over medium heat and add olive oil. Add the squash purée and the remaining ½ cup of milk. Simmer within 5 minutes. Add the cheese and stir to combine.
3. Add the pasta to the sauté pan and stir to combine. Serve immediately.

Nutrition:

Calories: 373 kcal; Protein: 14 g; Carbohydrate: 59 g; Fat: 10 g

★ ★ ★ ★ ★

Braised Kale

Preparation Time: 10 minutes | Cooking Time: 15 minutes

Servings: 3

Ingredients:

- 2 tbsp water
- 1 tbsp coconut oil
- 2 stalk celery (sliced to 1/4-inch thick)
- 5 cups kale, chopped

Directions:

1. Heat a pan over medium heat.
2. Add coconut oil and sauté the celery for at least 5 minutes.
3. Add the kale.
4. Add a tbsp of water.
5. Let the vegetables wilt for a few minutes. Add a tbsp of water if the kale starts to stick to the pan.
6. Serve warm.

Nutrition:

Calories: 81 kcal; Protein: 1 g; Carbohydrates: 3 g; Fat: 5 g

★ ★ ★ ★ ★

Black-Eyed Peas and Greens Power Salad

Preparation Time: 15 minutes | Cooking Time: 6 minutes

Servings: 2

Ingredients:

- 1 tbsp olive oil
- 3 cups purple cabbage, chopped
- 5 cups baby spinach

- 1 cup carrots, shredded
- 1 can black-eyed peas, drained
- Salt
- Black pepper, freshly ground

Directions:

1. In a medium pan, add the oil and cabbage and sauté for 1 to 2 minutes on medium heat. Add in your spinach, and cover for 3 to 4 minutes on medium heat, until greens are wilted. Remove from the heat and add to a large bowl.

2. Add in the carrots and black-eyed peas. Season with salt and pepper, if desired. Toss and serve.

Nutrition:

Calories: 320 kcal; Protein: 16 g; Carbohydrate: 49 g; Fat: 9 g

★ ★ ★ ★ ★

Baked Chickpea-And-Rosemary Omelet

Preparation Time: 15 minutes | Cooking Time: 15 minutes

Servings: 2

Ingredients:

- 1/2 tbsp olive oil
- 4 eggs
- 1/4 cup Parmesan cheese, grated
- 1 (15 oz.) can chickpeas, drained and rinsed
- 2 cups packed baby spinach
- 1 cup button mushrooms, chopped
- 2 sprigs rosemary, leaves picked (or 2 tsp dried rosemary)
- Salt
- Black pepper, freshly ground

Directions:

1. Warm oven to 400°F and puts a baking tray on the middle shelf. Line an 8-inch springform pan with baking paper and grease generously with olive oil. If you don't have a springform pan, grease an oven-safe skillet (or cast-iron skillet) with olive oil.
2. Lightly whisk the eggs and Parmesan. Place chickpeas in the prepared pan. Layer the spinach and mushrooms on top of the beans. Pour the egg mixture on top and scatter the rosemary. Season to taste with salt and pepper.
3. Place the pan on the preheated tray and bake until golden and puffy and the center feels firm and springy about 15 minutes. Remove from the oven, slice, and serve immediately.

Nutrition:

Calories: 418 kcal; Protein: 20 g; Carbohydrate: 33 g; Fat: 12 g

★ ★ ★ ★ ★

Chilled Cucumber-And-Avocado Soup with Dill

Preparation Time: 15 minutes | Cooking Time: 30 minutes

Servings: 4

Ingredients:

- 2 English cucumbers, peeled and diced, plus 1/4 cup reserved for garnish
- 1 avocado, peeled, pitted, and chopped, plus 1/4 cup reserved for garnish
- 1 1/2 cups non-fat or low-fat plain Greek yogurt
- 1/2 cup cold water
- 1/3 cup loosely packed dill, plus sprigs for garnish
- 1/4 tsp black pepper, freshly ground
- 1/4 tsp salt

Directions:

1. Purée ingredients in a blender until smooth. If you prefer a thinner soup, add more water until you reach the desired consistency. Divide soup among 4 bowls.
2. Cover with plastic wrap and refrigerate within 30 minutes. Garnish with cucumber, avocado, and dill sprigs, if desired.

Nutrition:

Calories: 142 kcal; Protein: 11 g; Carbohydrate: 12 g; Fat: 7 g

Grains, Beans, And Legumes

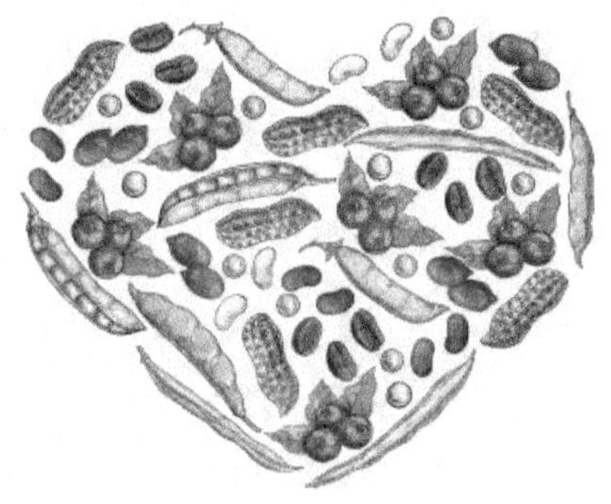

Quinoa a la Puttanesca

Preparation Time: 20 minutes | Cooking Time: 15 minutes

Servings: 4

Ingredients:

- 1 cup brown quinoa
- 2 cups water
- Sea salt to taste
- 4 cups zucchini, diced
- 4 pitted green olives, sliced
- 4 Kalamata olives, sliced
- 1 1/2 tbsp capers
- 1 tbsp olive oil
- 1 tbsp parsley, chopped
- 1/4 cup basil, chopped

Directions:

1. Add quinoa, water, and salt to a medium pot and cook for 15 minutes. In a bowl, mix zucchini, green olives, olives, capers, olive oil, parsley, and basil.
2. Allow sitting for 5 minutes. Serve.

Nutrition:

Calories: 231 kcal; Protein: 12 g; Carbohydrates: 35 g; Fat: 7 g

★ ★ ★ ★ ★

Hot Paprika Lentils

Preparation Time: 10 minutes | Cooking Time: 20 minutes

Servings: 6

Ingredients:

- 1 tbsp olive oil
- 1 tbsp hot paprika
- 2 1/4 cups lentils, drained
- 1/2 tsp thyme, dried
- Salt and black pepper, to taste

Directions:

1. Heat the oil in your pot over medium heat.
2. Sauté for 3 minutes. Add in paprika, salt, pepper, 5 cups water, lentils, and thyme.
3. Bring to a boil, lower the heat and simmer for 15 minutes, stirring often.

Nutrition:

Calories: 111 kcal; Protein: 11 g; Carbohydrates: 9 g; Fat: 6 g

Tender Farro

Preparation Time: 8 minutes | Cooking Time: 40 minutes

Servings: 4

Ingredients:

- 1 cup farro
- 3 cups beef broth
- 1 tsp salt
- 1 tbsp almond butter

- 1 tbsp dried dill

Directions:

1. Place farro in the pan.
2. Add beef broth, dried dill, and salt.
3. Close the lid and place the mixture to boil.
4. Then boil it for 35 minutes over medium-low heat.
5. When the time is done, open the lid and add almond butter.
6. Mix up the cooked farro well.

Nutrition:

Calories: 95 kcal; Protein: 6.4 g; Carbohydrates: 10.1 g; Fat: 3.3 g

Chicken Green Beans Soup

Preparation Time: 5 minutes | Cooking Time: 25 minutes

Servings: 4

Ingredients:

- 1 lb. chicken breasts, boneless, skinless, cubed
- 1 1/2 cups celery, chopped
- 1 tbsp olive oil
- 1 cup carrots, chopped
- 1 cup green beans, chopped
- 3 tbsp flour
- 1 tsp oregano, dried
- 2 tsp basil, dried
- 1/4 tsp nutmeg
- 1 tsp thyme
- 32 oz. chicken broth
- 1/2 cup almond milk
- 2 cups green peas, frozen
- 1/4 tsp black pepper

Directions:

1. Add the chicken to a skillet and sauté for 6 minutes, then remove it from the heat.
2. Warm up the olive oil in a pan and stir in the carrots, flour, green beans, basil, sautéed chicken, thyme, oregano, and nutmeg.
3. Sauté for approximately 3 minutes, then transfer the ingredients to a large pan.
4. Add the milk and broth and cook until it boils.
5. Stir in the green peas and cook for 5 minutes.
6. Adjust seasoning with pepper and serve warm.

Nutrition:

Calories: 277 kcal; Protein: 25.5 g; Carbohydrates: 17.3 g; Fat: 7.6 g

Brown Rice Pilaf

Preparation Time: 5 minutes | Cooking Time: 10 minutes

Servings: 4

Ingredients:

- 1 cup low-sodium vegetable broth
- 1/2 tbsp olive oil
- 1 scallion, thinly sliced
- 1 cup instant brown rice
- 1/8 tsp black pepper, freshly ground

Directions:

1. Mix the vegetable broth, olive oil, and scallion in a saucepan and boil. Put rice, then boil it again, adjust the heat and simmer within 10 minutes.
2. Remove and let stand within 5 minutes. Fluff with a fork then season with black pepper.

Nutrition:

Calories: 100 kcal; Protein: 2 g; Carbohydrate: 19 g; Fat: 2 g

★ ★ ★ ★ ★

Southern Bean Bowl

Preparation Time: 15 minutes | Cooking Time: 0 minutes

Servings: 4

Ingredients:

- 1 zucchini, chopped
- 1 red bell pepper, chopped
- 1green bell pepper, chopped
- 1 (14 1/2 oz./411 g) can black-eyed peas
- 1 (14 1/2 oz./411 g) can black beans
- 1/4 cup capers
- 2 avocados, pitted
- 1/4 cup sake
- 1 tsp oregano, dried
- Sea salt, to taste
- 1 tbsp olive oil
- 1 cup leafy greens, chopped

Directions:

1. In a bowl, mix the zucchini, peppers, black-eyed peas, beans, and capers.
2. Put the avocados, sake, olive oil, oregano, and salt in a food processor and blitz until smooth. Add the dressing to the bean bowl and toss to combine.
3. Top with leafy greens to serve.

Nutrition:

Calories: 412 kcal; Protein: 7 g; Carbohydrates: 48 g; Fat: 16 g

★ ★ ★ ★ ★

Hot Coconut Beans with Vegetables

Preparation Time: 15 minutes | Cooking Time: 10 minutes

Servings: 4

Ingredients:

- 2 tbsp olive oil
- 1 red bell pepper, chopped
- 1 tbsp hot powder
- 1 (13 1/2 oz./383 g) can coconut milk
- 2 (15 1/2 oz./439 g) cans white beans
- 1 (14 1/2 oz./411 g) can zucchini, diced
- 3 cups fresh baby spinach
- Sea salt and pepper, to taste
- Walnuts, chopped and toasted

Directions:

1. Heat the oil in your pot over medium heat. Place in hot powder, and bell pepper and sauté for 5 minutes, stirring occasionally.
2. Put in the coconut milk and whisk until well mixed.
3. Add in white beans, zucchini, spinach, salt, and pepper, and cook for 5 minutes until the spinach wilts.
4. Garnish with walnuts and serve.

Nutrition:

Calories: 578 kcal; Protein: 11 g; Carbohydrates: 48 g; Fat: 38 g

★ ★ ★ ★ ★

Quinoa Salmon Bowl

Preparation Time: 15 minutes | Cooking Time: 0 minutes

Servings: 4

Ingredients:

- 4 cups cooked quinoa
- 1 lb. (45g;) salmon, cooked and flaked
- 3 cups arugula
- 6 radishes, thinly sliced
- 1 zucchini, sliced into half moons
- 3 scallions, minced
- 2 tbsp almond oil
- 1 tbsp apple cider vinegar
- 1 tsp Sriracha or other hot sauce (or more if you like it spicy)
- 1 tsp salt
- 1/2 cup almonds, toasted and slivered (optional)

Directions:

1. Combine the quinoa, salmon, arugula, radishes, zucchini, and scallions in a large bowl.
2. Add the almond oil, vinegar, Sriracha, and salt and mix well.
3. Divide the mixture among four serving bowls, garnish with the toasted almonds (if using), and serve.

Nutrition:

Calories: 790 kcal; Protein: 37 g; Carbohydrates: 45 g; Fat: 22 g

★ ★ ★ ★ ★

Fiery Quinoa

Preparation Time: 10 minutes | Cooking Time: 20 minutes

Servings: 4

Ingredients:

- 1 cup quinoa, rinsed
- 2 cups water
- 1/2 cup coconut, shredded
- 1/4 cup hemp seeds
- 2 tbsp flaxseed
- 1 tsp cinnamon, ground
- 1 tsp vanilla extract
- Pinch sea salt
- 1 cup fresh berries of your choice, divided
- 1/4 cup hazelnuts, chopped

Directions:

1. Combine the quinoa and water in a medium saucepan over high heat.
2. Bring to a boil, then place the heat to a simmer, and cook for 15 to 20 minutes, or until the quinoa is cooked through. It should double or triple in bulk to couscous, and be slightly translucent.
3. Stir in the coconut, hemp seeds, flaxseed, cinnamon, vanilla, and salt.
4. Divide the quinoa among four bowls and top each serving with ¼ cup of berries and 1 tbsp of hazelnuts.

Nutrition:

Calories: 286 kcal; Protein: 10 g; Carbohydrates: 32 g; Fat: 13 g

★ ★ ★ ★ ★

Chunky Black-Bean Dip

Preparation Time: 5 minutes | Cooking Time: 1 minute

Servings: 2

Ingredients:

- 1 (15 oz.) can black beans, drained, with liquid reserved
- 1/2-can chipotle peppers in adobo sauce
- 1/4 cup plain Greek yogurt
- Black pepper, freshly ground

Directions:

1. Combine beans, peppers, and yogurt in a food processor or blender and process until smooth.
2. Add some of the bean liquid, 1 tbsp at a time, for a thinner consistency.
3. Season to taste with black pepper.
4. Serve.

Nutrition:

Calories: 70 kcal; Protein: 8 g; Carbohydrate: 11 g; Fat: 3 g

Asparagus Rice

Preparation Time: 20 minutes | Cooking Time: 10 minutes

Servings: 4

Ingredients:

- 3 large eggs, beaten
- 1/2 tsp ginger, ground
- 2 tsp low-sodium soy sauce
- 2 tbsp olive oil

- 1 cup cremini mushrooms, sliced
- 1 (10 oz.) package brown rice, frozen and thawed
- 8 oz. fresh asparagus, about 15 spears, cut into 1-inch pieces
- 1 tsp sesame oil

Directions:

1. Whisk the eggs, ginger, and soy sauce in a small bowl and set aside.
2. Heat the olive oil in a medium skillet or wok over medium heat.
3. Sauté for 2 minutes until tender-crisp.
4. Add the mushrooms and rice; stir-fry for 3 minutes longer.
5. Add the asparagus and fry for 2 minutes.
6. Move the rice mixture to one side of the skillet and pour in the egg mixture. Stir the eggs until cooked through, 2 to 3 minutes, and stir into the rice mixture.
7. Sprinkle the fried rice with the sesame oil and serve.

Nutrition:

Calories: 247 kcal; Protein: 9 g; Carbohydrates: 25 g; Fat: 13 g

Jalapeno Black-Eyed Peas Mix

Preparation Time: 10 minutes | Cooking Time: 5 hours

Servings: 12

Ingredients:

- 17 oz. black-eyed peas
- 1 sweet red pepper, chopped
- 1 jalapeno, chopped
- 6 cups water
- 1/2 tsp cumin, ground

- A pinch black pepper
- 2 tbsp cilantro, chopped

Directions:

1. In a slow cooker, mix the peas with the red pepper, jalapeno, black pepper, cumin, water, and cilantro, cover, and cook low for 5 hours.
2. Serve.

Nutrition:

Calories: 75 kcal; Protein: 4.3 g; Carbohydrates: 7.2 g; Fat: 3.5 g

Vegan Bean Mix

Preparation Time: 10 minutes | Cooking Time: 0 minutes

Servings:

INGREDIENTS:

- 1 cup lettuce, chopped
- 1 cucumber, chopped
- 1/2 cup corn kernels, cooked
- 1/2 cup fresh parsley, chopped
- 1 cup black beans, cooked

DIRECTION:

1. Put all ingredients in the mixing bowl and carefully mix.
2. Then transfer the mix in the serving bowls.
3. Add olive oil, if desired.

NUTRITION:

Calories: 227; Protein: 9.3g; Fat: 19.3g

Stir-Fried Green Beans

Preparation Time: 10 minutes | Cooking Time: 20 minutes

Servings: 3

INGREDIENTS:

- 1-pound green beans
- 1 tablespoon olive oil
- 1 teaspoon allspices
- 1/4 cup of water
- 1 teaspoon apple cider vinegar

DIRECTION:

1. Chop the green beans roughly and put them in the hot saucepan.
2. Add water and cook the vegetables for 10 minutes on low heat.
3. Add olive oil, allspices, and stir well.
4. Cook the green beans for 10 minutes more.
5. When the vegetables are soft, they are cooked.
6. Sprinkle the beans with apple cider vinegar and transfer in the plates.

NUTRITION:

Calories: 366; Protein: 12.3g; Carbs: 33.4g; Fat: 19.3g

★ ★ ★ ★ ★

Poultry

Healthy Chicken Orzo

Preparation Time: 15 minutes | Cooking Time: 15 minutes

Servings: 4

Ingredients:

- 1 cup whole wheat orzo
- 1 lb. chicken breasts, sliced
- 1/2 tsp red pepper flakes
- 1/2 cup feta cheese, crumbled
- 1/2 tsp oregano
- 1 tbsp fresh parsley, chopped
- 1 tbsp fresh basil, chopped
- 1/4 cup pine nuts
- 1 cup spinach, chopped
- 1/4 cup white wine
- 1/2 cup olives, sliced
- 1 cup zucchini, cut in half
- 2 tbsp olive oil
- 1/2 tsp pepper
- 1/2 tsp salt

Directions:

1. Add water to a small saucepan and bring to boil. Heat 1 tbsp of olive oil in a pan over medium heat. Season chicken with pepper and salt and cook in the pan for 5–7 minutes on each side. Remove from pan and set aside.

2. Add orzo to boiling water and cook according to the packet directions. Heat remaining olive oil in a pan on medium heat, then sauté for a minute. Stir in white wine and zucchini and cook on high for 3 minutes.

3. Add cooked orzo, spices, spinach, pine nuts, and olives and stir until well combined. Add chicken on top of orzo and sprinkle with feta cheese. Serve and enjoy.

Nutrition:

Calories: 518 kcal; Fat: 12.7 g; Protein: 20.6 g; Carbs: 26.2 g

★ ★ ★ ★ ☆

Mediterranean Turkey Breast

Preparation Time: 15 minutes | Cooking Time: 4 minutes and 30 minutes | Servings: 6

Ingredients:

- 4 lb. turkey breast
- 3 tbsp flour
- 3/4 cup chicken stock
- 1 tsp oregano, dried
- 1/2 cup zucchini, chopped
- 1/2 cup olives, chopped
- 1/4 tsp pepper
- 1/2 tsp salt

Directions:

1. Add turkey breast, oregano, zucchini, olives, pepper, and salt to the slow cooker. Add half stock. Cook on high within 4 hours.
2. Whisk remaining stock and flour in a small bowl and add to slow cooker. Cover and cook for 30 minutes more. Serve and enjoy.

Nutrition:

Calories: 537 kcal; Fat: 9.7 g; Protein: 59.1 g; Carbs: 29.6 g

★ ★ ★ ★ ☆

Chicken

Preparation Time: 15 minutes | Cooking Time: 12 minutes

Servings: 3

Ingredients:

- 3 chicken breasts, cut into thin slices
- 2 tbsp olive oil
- Pepper
- Salt

Directions:

1. Warm-up olive oil in a pan over medium heat. Sauté for 30 seconds. Put the chicken in the pan and sauté within 10 minutes. Bring to boil. Remove from heat and season with pepper and salt. Serve and enjoy.

Nutrition:

Calories: 439 kcal; Fat: 17.8 g; Protein: 42.9 g; Carbs: 4.9 g

★ ★ ★ ★ ★

Chicken adobo

Preparation time: 10 minutes | Cooking time: 15 minutes

Serving: 4

INGREDIENTS:

- 3 tbsp. Extra-virgin olive oil
- 1 1/2 pounds boneless skinless chicken breasts, cut into bite-size pieces
- 2 tsp. Ground turmeric
- 1/4 c. Low-sodium soy sauce
- 1/2 tsp. Sea salt
- 1/4 tsp. Freshly ground black pepper

DIRECTIONS:

1. In a large nonstick skillet over medium to high heat, heat the olive oil until it shimmers.
2. Add the chicken and turmeric. Cook for like 7 to 10 minutes, stirring occasionally, until the chicken is cooked through.
3. Stir in the soy sauce, salt, and pepper. Cook for 3 minutes, stirring.

Ingredient tip:

let's talk about freshly ground black pepper. While it's not a requirement in these recipes, grinding black peppercorns fresh produces a lot more flavor. Plus, grinding pepper makes your cooking feel more immediate, like you're a celebrity chef prepping food on tv. You can even find peppercorns in a disposable grinder in the spice aisle of your local grocery store.

NUTRITION (PER SERVING):

Calories: 498 Total fat: 22 g Total carbs: 11 Protein: 46 g.

Chicken and bell pepper sauté

Preparation time: 15 minutes | Cooking time: 15 minutes

Serving: 4

INGREDIENTS:

- 3 tbsp. Extra-virgin olive oil
- 1 red bell pepper, chopped
- 1 1/2 pounds boneless, skinless chicken breasts, cut into bite-size pieces
- 1/2 tsp. Sea salt
- 1/4 tsp. Freshly ground black pepper

DIRECTIONS:

1. In a large nonstick skillet over medium-high heat, heat the olive oil until it shimmers.
2. Add the red bell pepper and chicken. Cook for 10 minutes, stirring it occasionally.
3. Add salt and pepper. Cook for 30 seconds, stirring constantly.

Ingredient tip:

remember, smaller pieces cook faster. Cut the chicken and veggies into samesize pieces (1/2 to 1 inch) so they cook evenly.

NUTRITION (PER SERVING):

Calories: 279 Total fat: 13 g Protein: 23

★ ★ ★ ★ ★

Baked Chicken

Preparation Time: 15 minutes | Cooking Time: 35 minutes

Servings: 4

Ingredients:

- 2 lb. chicken tenders
- 2 large zucchini
- 2 tbsp olive oil
- 3 dill sprigs

For topping:

- 2 tbsp low-fat feta cheese, crumbled
- 1 tbsp olive oil
- 1 tbsp fresh dill, chopped

Directions:

1. Warm oven to 200°C/400°F. Drizzle the olive oil on a baking tray, then place chicken, zucchini, and dill, on the tray. Season

with salt. Bake chicken within 30 minutes.

2. Meanwhile, in a small bowl, stir all topping ingredients. Place chicken on the serving tray, then top with veggies and discard dill sprigs. Sprinkle topping mixture on top of chicken and vegetables. Serve and enjoy.

Nutrition:

Calories: 557 kcal; Fat: 23.6 g; Protein: 47.9 g; Carbs: 5.2 g

★ ★ ★ ★ ★

Simple Mediterranean Chicken

Preparation Time: 15 minutes | Cooking Time: 15 minutes

Servings: 3

Ingredients:

- 2 chicken breasts, skinless and boneless
- 1 1/2 cup zucchini, cut in half
- 1/2 cup olives
- 2 tbsp olive oil
- 1 tsp Italian seasoning
- 1/4 tsp pepper
- 1/4 tsp salt

Directions:

1. Season chicken with Italian seasoning, pepper, and salt. Warm-up olive oil in a pan over medium heat. Add season chicken to the pan and cook for 4–6 minutes on each side. Transfer chicken to a plate.
2. Put zucchini plus olives in the pan and cook for 2–4 minutes. Pour olive and zucchini mixture on top of the chicken and serve.

Nutrition:

Calories: 468 kcal; Fat: 19.4 g; Protein: 33.8 g; Carbs: 7.8 g

★ ★ ★ ★ ★

Pepper Chicken

Preparation Time: 15 minutes | Cooking Time: 21 minutes

Servings: 2

Ingredients:

- 2 chicken breasts, cut into strips
- 2 bell peppers, cut into strips
- 3 tbsp water
- 2 tbsp olive oil
- 1 tbsp paprika
- 1 tsp black pepper
- 1/2 tsp salt

Directions:

1. Warm-up olive oil in a large saucepan over medium heat. Sauté for 2–3 minutes. Add peppers and cook for 3 minutes. Add chicken and spices and stir to coat. Add water and stir well. Bring to boil. Cover and simmer for 10–15 minutes. Serve and enjoy.

Nutrition:

Calories: 462 kcal; Fat: 20.7 g; Protein: 44.7 g; Carbs: 14.8 g

★ ★ ★ ★ ★

Mustard Chicken Tenders

Preparation Time: 15 minutes | Cooking Time: 20 minutes

Servings: 4

Ingredients:

- 1 lb. chicken tenders
- 2 tbsp fresh tarragon, chopped
- 1/2 cup whole grain mustard
- 1/2 tsp paprika
- 1/2 tsp pepper
- 1/4 tsp kosher salt

Directions:

1. Warm oven to 425°F. Add all ingredients except chicken to the large bowl and mix well. Put the chicken in the bowl, then stir until well coated. Place chicken on a baking dish and cover. Bake within 15–20 minutes. Serve and enjoy.

Nutrition:

Calories: 242 kcal; Fat: 9.5 g; Protein: 33.2 g; Carbs: 3.1 g

Honey Crusted Chicken

Preparation Time: 10 minutes | Cooking Time: 25 minutes

Servings: 2

Ingredients:

- 1 tsp paprika
- 8 saltine crackers, 2 inches square
- 2 chicken breasts, each 4 oz.
- 4 tsp honey

Directions:

1. Set the oven to heat at 375°F. Grease a baking dish with cooking oil. Smash the crackers in a Ziplock bag and toss them with paprika in a bowl. Brush chicken with honey and add it to the crackers.
2. Mix well and transfer the chicken to the baking dish. Bake the chicken for 25 minutes until golden brown. Serve.

Nutrition:

Calories: 219 kcal; Fat: 17 g; Carbs: 12.1 g; Protein: 31 g

★ ★ ★ ★ ★

Chicken Sliders

Preparation Time: 10 minutes | Cooking Time: 10 minutes

Servings: 4

Ingredients:

- 10 oz. chicken breast, ground
- 1 tbsp black pepper
- 1 tbsp balsamic vinegar
- 1 tbsp fennel seed, crushed
- 4 whole-wheat mini buns
- 4 lettuce leaves
- 4 zucchini slices

Directions:

1. Combine all the ingredients except the wheat buns, zucchini, and lettuce. Mix well and refrigerate the mixture for 1 hour. Divide the mixture into 4 patties.
2. Broil these patties in a greased baking tray until golden brown. Place the chicken patties in the wheat buns along with lettuce and zucchini. Serve.

Nutrition:

Calories: 224 kcal; Fat: 4.5 g; Carbs: 10.2 g; Protein: 67.4 g

★ ★ ★ ★ ★

Apricot Chicken

Preparation Time: 15 minutes | Cooking Time: 6 minutes

Servings: 4

Ingredients:

- 1 bottle creamy French dressing
- 1/4 cup flavorless oil
- White rice, cooked
- 1 large jar Apricot preserve
- 4 lb. chicken, boneless and skinless

Directions:

1. Rinse and pat dry the chicken. Dice into bite-size pieces. In a large bowl, mix the apricot preserve and creamy dressing. Stir until thoroughly combined. Place the chicken in the bowl. Mix until coated.
2. In a large skillet, heat the oil. Place the chicken in the oil gently. Cook 4–6 minutes on each side, until golden brown. Serve over rice.

Nutrition:

Calories: 202 kcal; Fat: 12 g; Carbs: 75 g; Protein: 20 g

★ ★ ★ ★ ★

Buffalo Chicken Salad Wrap

Preparation Time: 10 minutes | Cooking Time: 10 minutes

Servings: 4

Ingredients:

- 3–4 oz. chicken breasts
- 2 whole chipotle peppers
- 1/4 cup white wine vinegar
- 1/4 cup low-calorie mayonnaise
- 2 stalks celery, diced
- 2 carrots, cut into matchsticks
- 1/2 cup rutabaga or another root vegetable, thinly sliced
- 4 oz. spinach, cut into strips
- 2 whole-grain tortillas (12-inch diameter)

Directions:

1. Set the oven or a grill to heat at 375°F. Bake the chicken first for 10 minutes per side. Blend chipotle peppers with mayonnaise and wine vinegar in the blender. Dice the baked chicken into cubes or small chunks.

2. Mix the chipotle mixture with all the ingredients except tortillas and spinach. Spread 2 oz. of spinach over the tortilla and scoop the stuffing on top. Wrap the tortilla and cut it in half. Serve.

Nutrition:

Calories: 300 kcal; Fat: 16.4 g; Carbs: 8.7 g; Protein: 38.5 g

★ ★ ★ ★ ★

Rosemary Roasted Chicken

Preparation Time: 15 minutes | Cooking Time: 20 minutes

Servings: 8

Ingredients:

- 8 rosemary springs
- Black pepper
- 1 tbsp rosemary, chopped
- 1 chicken
- 1 tbsp organic olive oil

Directions:

1. In a bowl, mix rosemary, rub the chicken with black pepper, the oil, and rosemary mix, place it inside a roasting pan, introduce it inside the oven at 350°F, and roast for sixty minutes and 20 min. Carve chicken, divide between plates and serve using a side dish. Enjoy!

Nutrition:

Calories: 325 kcal; Fat: 5 g; Carbs: 15 g; Protein: 14 g

Artichoke and Spinach Chicken

Preparation Time: 15 minutes | Cooking Time: 5 minutes

Servings: 4

Ingredients:

- 10 oz. baby spinach
- 1/2 tsp red pepper flakes, crushed
- 14 oz. artichoke hearts, chopped
- 28 oz. no-salt-added sauce
- 2 tbsp Essential olive oil

- 4 chicken breasts, boneless and skinless

Directions:

1. Heat up a pan with the oil over medium-high heat, add chicken and red pepper flakes and cook for 5 minutes on them. Add spinach, artichokes, and sauce, toss, cook for ten minutes more, divide between plates and serve. Enjoy!

Nutrition:

Calories: 212 kcal; Fat: 3 g; Carbs: 16 g; Protein: 20 g

☆ ☆ ☆ ☆ ☆

Thai Chicken Thighs

Preparation Time: 15 minutes | Cooking Time: 1 hour and 5 minutes

Servings: 6

Ingredients:

- 1/2 cup Thai sauce
- 4 lb. chicken thighs

Directions:

1. Heat a pan over medium-high heat. Add chicken thighs, brown them for 5 minutes on both sides Transfer to some baking dish, then toss.
2. Introduce within the oven and bake at 400°F for 60 minutes. Divide everything between plates and serve. Enjoy!

Nutrition:

Calories: 220 kcal; Fat: 4 g; Carbs: 12 g; Protein: 10 g

☆ ☆ ☆ ☆ ☆

Oregano Chicken Thighs

Preparation Time: 15 minutes | Cooking Time: 20 minutes

Servings: 6

Ingredients:

- 12 chicken thighs
- 1 tsp parsley, dried
- 1/4 tsp pepper and salt
- 1/2 cup extra virgin essential olive oil
- 1 cup oregano, chopped
- 1/4 cup low-sodium veggie stock

Directions:

1. In your food processor, mix parsley with oregano, salt, pepper, and stock and pulse. Put chicken thighs within the bowl, add oregano paste, toss, cover, and then leave aside within the fridge for 10 minutes.
2. Heat the kitchen grill over medium heat, add chicken pieces, close the lid and cook for twenty or so minutes with them. Divide between plates and serve!

Nutrition:

Calories: 254 kcal; Fat: 3 g; Carbs: 7 g; Protein: 17 g

Fish and Seafood

Grilled Salmon with Edamame Beans

Preparation Time: 10 minutes | Cooking Time: 14 minutes

Servings: 3

INGREDIENTS:

- 1-pound salmon fillet
- 1/2 teaspoon thyme
- 1/2 teaspoon ground coriander
- 1 tablespoon olive oil
- 1/4 cup edamame beans, boiled
- 1 tablespoon mustard

DIRECTION:

1. Make a horizontal cut in the salmon and fill it with edamame beans.
2. Then secure the cut with toothpicks.
3. After this, gently rub the fish with thyme, ground coriander, olive oil, and mustard.
4. Preheat the grill to 390F.
5. Put the fish in the preheated grill and cook it for 7 minutes per side.

NUTRITION:

Calories: 215; Protein: 12.3g; Carbs: 33.4g; Fat: 19.3g

★ ★ ★ ★ ★

Fresh Tuna Steak and Fennel Salad

Preparation Time: 15 minutes | Cooking Time: 25 minutes

Servings: 2

Ingredients:

- 2 (1 inch) tuna steaks

- 2 tbsp olive oil, 1 tbsp olive oil for brushing
- 1 tsp black peppercorns, crushed
- 1 tsp fennel seeds, crushed
- 1 fennel bulb, trimmed and sliced
- 1/2 cup water
- 1 tsp fresh parsley, chopped

Directions:

1. Coat the fish with oil and then season with peppercorns and fennel seeds.
2. Heat the oil on medium heat and sauté the fennel bulb slices for 5 minutes or until light brown.
3. Add the water to the pan and cook for 10 minutes until the fennel is tender.
4. Lower the heat to a simmer.
5. Meanwhile, heat another skillet and sauté the tuna steaks for about 2 to 3 minutes on each side for medium-rare. (Add 1 minute each side for medium and 2 minutes each side for medium well).
6. Serve the fennel mix with the tuna steaks on top and garnish with fresh parsley.

Nutrition:

Calories: 288 kcal; Protein: 44 g; Carbohydrates: 6 g; Fat: 9 g

Pan-Seared Haddock with Beets

Preparation Time: 20 minutes | Cooking Time: 30 minutes

Servings: 4

Ingredients:

- 8 beets, peeled and cut into eighths

- 2 shallots, thinly sliced
- 2 tbsp olive oil, divided
- 2 tbsp apple cider vinegar
- 1 tsp fresh thyme, chopped
- Pinch sea salt
- 4 (5 oz./142 g) haddock fillets, patted dry

Directions:

1. Preheat the oven to 400°F (205°C).
2. In a medium bowl, toss together the beets, shallots, and 1 tbsp of olive oil until well coated. Spread the beet mixture in a 9-by-13-inch baking dish. Roast for about 30 minutes, or until the vegetables are caramelized and tender.
3. Remove the beets from the oven and stir in the cider vinegar, thyme, and sea salt.
4. While the beets are roasting, place a large skillet over medium-high heat and add the remaining 1 tbsp of olive oil.
5. Panfry the fish for about 15 minutes, turning once, until it flakes when pressed with a fork. Serve the fish with a generous scoop of roasted beets.

Storage:

Store in an airtight container in the fridge for up to 4 days or in the freezer for up to 1 month.

Reheat:

Microwave covered, until the desired temperature is reached.

Nutrition:

Calories: 314 kcal; Protein: 28 g; Carbohydrates: 21 g; Fat: 9 g

Shrimp Mushroom Squash

Preparation Time: 10 minutes | Cooking Time: 20 minutes

Servings: 4

Ingredients:

- 2 tbsp hemp seeds
- 2 tbsp olive oil
- 1 lb. shrimp, peeled and deveined
- 1/4 cup coconut aminos
- 2 tbsp raw honey
- 2 tsp sesame oil
- 4 oz. shiitake mushrooms, (cut into slices)
- 1 red bell pepper, (cut into slices)
- 1 yellow squash, peeled and cubed
- 2 cups chard, chopped

Directions:

1. In a bowl (medium size), mix the aminos, honey, sesame oil, and hemp seeds.
2. In a skillet (you can also use a saucepan); heat the oil over the medium stove flame.
3. Stir the mixture and cook while stirring for about 2–3 minutes until softened.
4. Add the bell pepper, squash, and mushrooms, and stir-cook for 5 minutes.
5. Add the shrimp and aminos mix; stir-cook for 4 minutes more.
6. Add the chard, toss; add into serving bowls and serve.

Nutrition:

Calories: 236 kcal; Protein: 9 g; Carbohydrates: 11 g; Fat: 8 g

★ ★ ★ ★ ★

Spinach Sea Bass Lunch

Preparation Time: 10 minutes | Cooking Time: 30 minutes

Servings: 2

Ingredients:

- 2 sea bass fillets, boneless
- 2 shallots, chopped
- 5 zucchini, halved
- 1 tbsp parsley, chopped
- 1 tbsp olive oil
- 8 oz. baby spinach

Directions:

1. Preheat an oven to 450°F. Grease a baking dish with cooking spray.
2. Add the fish, zucchini, and parsley.
3. Cover the dish and bake for 12–15 minutes and add to serving plates.
4. In a skillet (you can also use a saucepan); heat the oil over the medium stove flame.
5. Add the shallots, stir the mixture and cook while stirring for about 1–2 minutes until softened.
6. Add the spinach, stir, and cook for 4–5 minutes more. Add with the fish and serve warm.

Nutrition:

Calories: 218 kcal; Protein: 18 g; Carbohydrates: 10 g Fat: 11 g

★ ★ ★ ★ ★

Cod Meal

Preparation Time: 5 minutes | Cooking Time: 35 minutes

Servings: 4

Ingredients:

- 2 tbsp olive oil
- 2 tbsp tarragon, chopped
- 1/4 cup parsley, chopped
- 4 cod fillets, skinless
- Black pepper and salt, ground, to the taste
- 1 tbsp thyme, chopped
- 4 cups water

Directions:

1. In a skillet (you can also use a saucepan); heat the oil over the medium stove flame.
2. Stir the mixture, and cook while stirring for about 2–3 minutes until softened.
3. Add the salt, pepper, tarragon, parsley, thyme, water.
4. Boil the mix; add the cod, cook for 12–15 minutes, and drain the liquid.
5. Serve with a side salad.

Nutrition:

Calories: 181 kcal; Protein: 12 g; Carbohydrates: 9 g; Fat: 3 g

★ ★ ★ ★ ★

Halibut in Parchment with Zucchini, Shallots, and Herbs

Preparation Time: 15 minutes | Cooking Time: 15 minutes

Servings: 4

Ingredients:

- 1/2 cup zucchini, diced small
- 1 shallot, minced
- 4 (5 oz.) halibut fillets (about 1 inch thick)
- 4 tsp extra-virgin olive oil
- 1/4 tsp kosher salt
- 1/8 tsp black pepper, freshly ground
- 8 sprigs thyme

Directions:

1. Preheat the oven to 450°F. Combine the zucchini and shallots in a medium bowl. Cut 4 (15-by-24-inch) pieces of parchment paper. Fold each sheet in half horizontally.
2. Draw a large half heart on one side of each folded sheet, with the fold along the heart center. Cut out the heart, open the parchment, and lay it flat.
3. Place a fillet near the center of each parchment heart. Drizzle 1 tsp olive oil on each fillet. Sprinkle with salt and pepper. Top each fillet with 2 sprigs of thyme. Sprinkle each fillet with one-quarter of the zucchini and shallot mixture. Fold the parchment over.
4. Starting at the top, fold the parchment edges over, and continue all the way around to make a packet. Twist the end tightly to secure. Arrange the 4 packets on a baking sheet. Bake for about 15 minutes. Place on plates; cut open. Serve immediately.

Nutrition:

Calories: 190 kcal; Protein: 20 g; Carbohydrates: 5 g; Fat: 7 g

Grilled Mahi-Mahi with Artichoke Caponata

Preparation Time: 15 minutes | Cooking Time: 30 minutes

Servings: 4

Ingredients:

- 2 tbsp extra-virgin olive oil
- 2 celery stalks, diced
- 1/2 cup zucchini, chopped
- 1/4 cup white wine
- 2 tbsp white wine vinegar
- 1 can artichoke hearts, drained and chopped
- 1/4 cup green olives, pitted and chopped
- 1 tbsp capers, chopped
- 1/4 tsp red pepper flakes
- 2 tbsp fresh basil, chopped
- 4 (5 to 6 oz. each) skinless mahi-mahi fillets
- 1/2 tsp kosher salt
- 1/4 tsp black pepper, freshly ground
- Olive oil cooking spray

Directions:

1. Warm-up olive oil in a skillet over medium heat, then put the celery, and sauté for 4 to 5 minutes. Sauté for 30 seconds. Add the zucchini and cook within 2 to 3 minutes. Add the wine and vinegar to deglaze the pan, increasing the heat to medium-high.

2. Add the artichokes, olives, capers, and red pepper flakes and simmer, reducing the liquid by half, for about 10 minutes. Mix in the basil.

3. Season the mahi-mahi with salt and pepper. Heat a grill skillet or grill pan over mediumhigh heat and coat with olive oil cooking spray. Add the fish and cook within 4 to 5 minutes per side. Serve topped with the artichoke caponata.

Nutrition:

Calories: 245 kcal; Protein: 24 g; Carbohydrates: 10 g; Fat: 8 g

★ ★ ★ ★ ★

Flounder with Zucchini and Basil

Preparation Time: 15 minutes | Cooking Time: 20 minutes

Servings: 4

Ingredients:

- 1 lb. zucchini
- 2 tbsp extra-virgin olive oil
- 2 tbsp basil, cut into ribbons
- 1/2 tsp kosher salt
- 1/4 tsp black pepper, freshly ground
- 4 (5 to 6 oz.) flounder fillets

Directions:

1. Preheat the oven to 425°F.
2. Mix the zucchini, olive oil, basil, salt, and black pepper in a baking dish. Bake for 5 minutes.
3. Remove, then arrange the flounder on top of the zucchini mixture. Bake until the fish is cooked and begins to flake, around 10 to 15 minutes, depending on thickness.

Nutrition:

Calories: 215 kcal; Protein: 22 g; Carbohydrates: 6 g; Fat: 9 g

★ ★ ★ ★ ★

Cod and Cauliflower Chowder

Preparation Time: 15 minutes | Cooking Time: 40 minutes

Servings: 4

Ingredients:

- 2 tbsp extra-virgin olive oil
- 1 leek, sliced thinly
- 1 medium head cauliflower, coarsely chopped
- 1 tsp kosher salt
- 1/4 tsp black pepper, freshly ground
- 2 pints zucchini
- 2 cups no-salt-added vegetable stock
- 1/4 cup green olives, pitted and chopped
- 1 to 11/2 lb. cod
- 1/4 cup fresh parsley, minced

Directions:

1. Heat the olive oil in a Dutch oven or large pot over medium heat. Add the leek and sauté until lightly golden brown, about 5 minutes.
2. Sauté within 30 seconds. Add the cauliflower, salt, and black pepper and sauté for 2 to 3 minutes.
3. Add the zucchini and vegetable stock, increase the heat to high and boil, then turn the heat to low and simmer within 10 minutes.
4. Add the olives and mix. Add the fish, cover, and simmer for 20 minutes or until the fish is opaque and flakes easily. Gently mix in the parsley.

Nutrition:

Calories: 270 kcal; Protein: 18 g; Carbohydrates: 19 g; Fat: 10 g

★ ★ ★ ★ ★

Buttered Tuna Lettuce Wraps

Preparation Time: 10 minutes | Cooking Time: 0 minutes

Servings: 2

Ingredients:

- 1 cup almond butter
- 1 tsp low-sodium soy sauce
- 1/2 tsp sriracha, or to taste
- 1/2 cup water chestnuts, canned, drained, and chopped
- 2 (2.6 oz. / 74 g) packages tuna, packed in water, drained
- 2 large butter lettuce leaves

Directions:

1. Stir together the almond butter, soy sauce, and sriracha in a medium bowl until well mixed. Add the water chestnuts and tuna and stir until well incorporated.
2. Place 2 butter lettuce leaves on a flat work surface, spoon half of the tuna mixture onto each leaf and roll up into a wrap. Serve immediately.

Nutrition:

Calories: 270 kcal; Protein: 19 g; Carbohydrates: 18 g; Fat: 13 g

★ ★ ★ ★ ★

Tilapia with Limey Cilantro Salsa

Preparation Time: 5 minutes | Cooking Time: 10 minutes

Servings: 2

Ingredients: *Salsa:*

- 1 cup mango, chopped

- 2 tbsp fresh cilantro, chopped
- 2 tbsp lime juice, freshly squeezed
- 1/2 jalapeño pepper, seeded and minced
- Pinch salt

Tilapia:

- 1 tbsp paprika
- 1/2 tsp thyme, dried
- 1/2 tsp black pepper, freshly ground
- 1/4 tsp salt
- 1 lb. tilapia fillets, boneless
- 2 tsp extra-virgin olive oil
- 1 lime, cut into wedges, for serving

Directions:

1. **Make the salsa:** Place the mango, cilantro, lime juice, jalapeño, and salt in a medium bowl and toss to combine. Set aside.
2. **Make the tilapia:** Stir together the paprika, thyme, black pepper, pepper, and salt in a mini bowl until well mixed. Rub both sides of the fillets generously with the mixture.
3. Heat the olive oil in a huge skillet over medium heat.
4. Add the fish fillets and cook each side for 3 to 5 minutes until golden brown and cooked through.
5. Divide the fillets among 2 plates and spoon half of the prepared salsa onto each fillet.
6. Serve the fish alongside the lime wedges.

Nutrition:

Calories: 239 kcal; Protein: 25 g; Carbohydrates: 21 g; Fat: 7.8 g

★ ★ ★ ★ ★

Peppered Paprika with Grilled Sea Bass

Preparation Time: 20 minutes | Cooking Time: 20 minutes

Servings: 6

Ingredients:

- 1/4 tsp paprika
- Sea salt, to taste
- 2 lb. (90 g) sea bass
- 3 tbsp extra-virgin olive oil, divided
- 1 tbsp Italian flat leaf parsley, chopped

Directions:

1. Preheat the grill to high heat.
2. Place the paprika, and sea salt in a large bowl and stir to combine.
3. Dredge the fish in the spice mixture, turning until well coated.
4. Heat 2 tbsp of olive oil in a small skillet. Add the parsley and cook for 1 to 2 minutes, stirring occasionally. Remove the skillet from the heat and set it aside.
5. Brush the grill grates lightly with the remaining 1 tbsp olive oil.
6. Grill the fish for about 7 minutes. Flip the fish and cook for an additional 7 minutes, or until the fish flakes when pressed lightly with a fork.
7. Serve hot.

Nutrition:

Calories: 200 kcal; Protein: 26 g; Carbohydrates: 0.6 g; Fat: 10.3 g

Sardine Bruschetta with Fennel

Preparation Time: 15 minutes | Cooking Time: 0 minutes

Servings: 4

Ingredients:

- 1/4 cup low-fat Greek yogurt
- 1/3 tbsp light mayonnaise
- 3/4 tsp kosher salt, divided
- 1 fennel bulb, cored and thinly sliced
- 1/4 cup parsley, chopped, plus more for garnish
- 1/4 cup fresh mint, chopped
- 2 tsp extra-virgin olive oil
- 1/8 tsp black pepper, freshly ground
- 8 slices multigrain bread, toasted
- 2 (4.4 oz.) cans sardines, smoked

Directions:

1. Mix the yogurt, mayonnaise, and ¼ tsp of salt in a small bowl.
2. Mix the remaining ½ tsp salt, the fennel, parsley, mint, olive oil, and black pepper in a separate small bowl.
3. Spoon 1 tbsp of the yogurt mixture on each piece of toast. Divide the fennel mixture evenly on top of the yogurt mixture. Divide the sardines among the toasts, placing them on top of the fennel mixture. Garnish with more herbs, if desired.

Nutrition:

Calories: 400 kcal; Protein: 16 g; Carbohydrates: 51 g; Fat: 12 g

★ ★ ★ ★ ★

Chopped Tuna Salad

Preparation Time: 15 minutes | Cooking Time: 0 minutes

Servings: 4

Ingredients:

- 2 tbsp extra-virgin olive oil
- 2 tsp Dijon mustard
- 1/2 tsp kosher salt
- 1/4 tsp black pepper, freshly ground
- 12 olives, pitted and chopped
- 1/2 cup celery, diced
- 1/2 cup red bell pepper, diced
- 1/2 cup fresh parsley, chopped
- 2 (6 oz.) cans no-salt-added tuna, packed in water, drained
- 6 cups baby spinach

Directions:

1. Mix the olive oil, mustard, salt, and black pepper in a medium bowl.
2. Add in the olives, celery, bell pepper, and parsley, and mix well. Add the tuna and gently incorporate.
3. Divide the spinach evenly among 4 plates or bowls. Spoon the tuna salad evenly on top of the spinach.

Nutrition:

Calories: 220 kcal; Protein: 25 g; Carbohydrates: 7 g; Fat: 11 g

★ ★ ★ ★ ★

Caramelized Fennel and Sardines with Penne

Preparation Time: 15 minutes | Cooking Time: 30 minutes

Servings: 4

Ingredients:

- 8 oz. whole-wheat penne
- 2 tbsp extra-virgin olive oil
- 1 bulb fennel, cored and thinly sliced, plus 1/4 cup fronds
- 2 celery stalks, thinly sliced, plus 1/2 cup leaves
- 3/4 tsp kosher salt
- 1/4 tsp black pepper, freshly ground
- 2 (4.4 oz.) cans sardines, boneless/skinless, packed in olive oil, undrained

Directions:

1. Cook the penne, as stated in the package directions. Drain, reserving 1 cup of pasta water. Warm-up olive oil in a large skillet over medium heat, then put the fennel and celery and cook within 10 to 12 minutes. Cook within 1 minute.
2. Add the penne, reserved pasta water, salt, and black pepper. Adjust the heat to medium high and cook for 1 to 2 minutes.
3. Remove, then stir in the fennel fronds, and celery leaves. Break the sardines into bite-size pieces and gently mix them in, along with the oil they were packed in.

Nutrition:

Calories: 400 kcal; Protein: 22 g; Carbohydrates: 46 g; Fat: 15 g

★ ★ ★ ★ ★

Greek Baked Cod

Preparation Time: 9 minutes | Cooking Time: 13 minutes

Servings: 4

Ingredients:

- 1 1/2 lb. Cod fillet pieces (4–6 pieces)
- 1/4 cup fresh parsley leaves, chopped

For coating:

- 1/3 cup all-purpose flour
- 1 tsp coriander, ground
- 3/4 tsp sweet Spanish paprika
- 3/4 tsp cumin, ground
- 3/4 tsp salt
- 1/2 tsp black pepper

Directions:

1. Preheat the oven to 400°F.
2. Scourge olive oil, and melted butter, set aside.
3. In another shallow bowl, mix all-purpose flour, spices, salt, and pepper.
4. Pat the fish fillet dry, then dip the fish in the flour mixture, and brush off extra flour.
5. In a cast-iron skillet over medium-high heat, add 2 tbsp olive oil.
6. Once heated, add in the fish and sear on each side for color, but do not thoroughly cook, remove from heat.
7. Drizzle all over the fish fillets.
8. Bake for 10 minutes, until it begins to flake easily with a fork.
9. Allow the dish to cool completely.
10. Distribute among the containers, and store for 2–3 days.
11. To Serve: Reheat in the microwave for 1–2 minutes or until heated through.
12. Sprinkle chopped parsley. Enjoy!

Nutrition:

Calories: 321 kcal; Protein: 23 g; Carbohydrates: 14 g; Fat: 13 g

Green Goddess Crab Salad with Endive

Preparation Time: 15 minutes | Cooking Time: 10 minutes

Servings: 4

Ingredients:

- 1 lb. lump crabmeat
- 2/3 cup low-fat Greek yogurt
- 3 tbsp mayonnaise
- 3 tbsp fresh chives, chopped, plus additional for garnish
- 3 tbsp fresh parsley, chopped, plus extra for garnish
- 3 tbsp fresh basil, chopped, plus extra for garnish
- 1/2 tsp kosher salt
- 1/4 tsp black pepper, freshly ground
- 3 endives, ends cut off, and leaves separated

Directions:

1. In a medium bowl, combine the crab, yogurt, mayonnaise, chives, parsley, basil, salt, plus black pepper, and mix until well combined.
2. Place the endive leaves on 4 salad plates. Divide the crab mixture evenly on top of the endive. Garnish with additional herbs, if desired.

Nutrition:

Calories: 200 kcal; Protein: 25 g; Carbohydrates: 44 g; Fat: 7 g

Seared Scallops with Blood Orange Glaze

Preparation Time: 15 minutes | Cooking Time: 20 minutes

Servings: 4

Ingredients:

- 3 tbsp extra-virgin olive oil, divided
- 1/2 tsp kosher salt, divided
- 4 blood oranges, juiced
- 1 tsp blood orange zest
- 1/2 tsp red pepper flakes
- 1 lb. scallops, small side muscle removed
- 1/4 tsp black pepper, freshly ground
- 1/4 cup fresh chives, chopped

Directions:

1. Heat 1 tbsp of the olive oil in a small saucepan over medium-high heat. Add 1/4 tsp of the salt and sauté for 30 seconds.
2. Add the orange juice and zest, bring to a boil, reduce the heat to medium-low, and cook within 20 minutes, or until the liquid reduces by half and becomes a thicker syrup consistency. Remove and mix in the red pepper flakes.
3. Pat the scallops dry with a paper towel and season with the remaining 1/4 tsp salt and the black pepper. Heat the remaining 2 tbsp of olive oil in a large skillet on medium-high heat. Add the scallops gently and sear.
4. Cook on each side within 2 minutes. If cooking in 2 batches, use 1 tbsp of oil per batch.
5. Serve the scallops with the blood orange glaze and garnish with the chives.

Nutrition:

Calories: 140 kcal; Protein: 15 g; Carbohydrates: 12 g; Fat: 4 g

★ ★ ★ ★ ★

Tuna With Vegetable Mix

Preparation Time: 8 minutes | Cooking Time: 16 minutes

Servings: 4

Ingredients:

- 2 tbsp extra-virgin olive oil divided
- 1 tbsp rice vinegar
- 1 tsp kosher salt, divided
- 3/4 tsp Dijon mustard
- 3/4 tsp honey
- 4 oz. baby gold beets, thinly sliced
- 4 oz. fennel bulb, trimmed and thinly sliced
- 4 oz. baby turnips, thinly sliced
- 6 oz. Granny Smith apple, very thinly sliced
- 2 tsp sesame seeds, toasted
- 6 oz. tuna steaks
- 1/2 tsp black pepper
- 1 tbsp fennel fronds, torn

Directions:

1. Scourge 2 tbsp of oil, 1/2 a tsp of salt, honey, vinegar, and mustard.
2. Give the mixture a nice mix.
3. Add fennel, beets, apple, and turnips; mix and toss until everything is evenly coated.
4. Sprinkle with sesame seeds and toss well.
5. Using a cast-iron skillet, heat 2 tbsp of oil over high heat.
6. Carefully season the tuna with 1/2 a tsp of salt and pepper
7. Situate the tuna in the skillet and cook for 4 minutes, giving 1 1/2 minutes per side.
8. Remove the tuna and slice it up.
9. Place in containers with the vegetable mix.
10. Serve with the fennel mix, and enjoy!

Nutrition:

Calories: 443 kcal; Protein: 19.5 g; Carbohydrates: 19 g; Fat: 13.1 g

Salmon & Zucchini Skewers

Preparation time: 5 minutes | Cooking time: 15minutes

Servings:4

Ingredients

- 1 salmon fillet, cut into cubes
- 1 zucchini, thinly sliced lengthwise
- Salt and pepper to taste
- 4-5 zucchini for serving
- Parsley leaves for serving

Directions

1. Coat salmon and zucchini with spices and thread on wooden skewers.
2. Grill skewers for about 4-5 minutes per side until cooked and brown. 3. Once cooked remove from grill
3. Serve with fresh veggies.
4. Enjoy.

Nutrition

171"Calories", "Protein"23 g, "Carbohydrate" 7 g, "Fats" 5 g, "Sugar" 3 g

Baked Salmon Loaf

Preparation time: 10 minutes | Cooking time: 40 minutes

Servings:4

Ingredients

- 1 lb. salmon, ground
- 2 large egg
- 2 tbsps. Italian seasoning
- Salt and pepper, to taste
- 1/2 cup green peas

Directions

1. Mix all loaf ingredients in mixing bowl and press it in greased loaf pan evenly.
2. Preheat oven to 325 F.
3. Place loaf pan in preheated oven and bake loaf for about 30-40 minutes in preheated oven.
4. Once loaf is cooked remove from oven.
5. Serve with fresh salad and sauce.
6. Enjoy!

Nutrition

211"Calories", "Protein"27 g, "Carbohydrate" 6 g, "Fats" 7 g, "Sugar" 2 g

Creamy Salmon

Preparation time:10 minutes | Cooking time: 20 minutes

Servings:

Ingredients

- 1 salmon fillet cut into bite size

- 1 cup low fat Greek yogurt
- salt & pepper to taste
- 1 tsp. paprika powder
- 1 tsp. cumin seeds
- 2 tbsps. chopped parsley

Directions

1. Heat a non-stick pan over medium heat.
2. Add salmon cubes in pan and cook for 4-5 minutes until salmon is brown.
3. Add Greek yogurt and spices in pan, cook for about 3-4 minutes. 4. Once cooked remove from pan 5. Sprinkle parsley on top.

Nutrition

398"Calories", "Protein"40 g, "Carbohydrate" 12 g, "Fats" 11 g, "Sugar" 5 g

Baked Fish In Herbs

Preparation time: 10 minutes | Cooking time:15 minutes

Servings: 4

Ingredients

- 1 Whole fish, 2 lb.
- salt & pepper to taste
- 1 tsp. paprika powder
- 1 tsp. cumin seeds
- 4 tbsps. lime juice

Directions

1. Add all ingredients in a bowl and mix well.
2. Arrange fish in greased baking tray and top with spice mix.

3. Bake fish in an oven for about 40 minutes until cooked and brown on top.
4. Enjoy.

Nutrition

309"Calories", "Protein"47 g, "Carbohydrate" 5 g, "Fats" 10 g, "Sugar" 1 g

Grilled Salmon With Asparagus

Preparation time: 10 minutes | Cooking time:20 minutes

Servings: 2

Ingredients

- 2 salmon fillet
- 1 lb. baby asparagus, trimmed and peeled
- 2 zucchini
- 1 tbsp. Italian seasoning
- Salt and pepper, to taste
- Lettuce leaves

Directions

1. Rub salmon fillet, asparagus and zucchini with all spices.
2. Place veggies and salmon in electric grill and grill for about 5-8 minutes per side.
3. Drizzle pepper on top.
4. Serve and enjoy!

Nutrition

451"Calories", "Protein"70 g, "Carbohydrate" 9 g, "Fats" 14 g, "Sugar" 4 g

Salads

Buddha lunch bowl

Preparation time: 10 minutes | Cooking time:10 minutes

Servings: 2

INGREDIENTS

- 4-5 zucchini, sliced
- Salt and pepper to taste
- 1 cucumber sliced
- 4-5 radish, sliced
- 1 can chickpeas, rinsed
- 1 firm ripe avocado, diced
- 1/4 cup chopped fresh parsley

DIRECTIONS

1. Cut vegetables and arrange in a bowl.
2. Sprinkle salt and pepper on top.
3. Serve and enjoy!

NUTRITION:

336"calories", "protein"12 g, "carbohydrate" 43 g, "fats" 18 g

★ ★ ★ ★ ★

Greek salad with fresh vegetables

Preparation time: 10 minutes | Cooking time: minutes

Servings: 2

INGREDIENTS

- 1 cucumber sliced
- 5-8 zucchini, half
- 4-5 lettuce leaves, chopped
- 1 cup kidney beans, boil

- 1 cup low fat feta cheese, cubes

Dressing

- 3/4 tsp. Salt
- 1/2 tsp dried thyme
- 1/2 tsp paprika

DIRECTIONS

1. Mix dressing ingredients in bowl.
2. Add cucumber, zucchini, lettuce leaves, beans, and cheese in serving bowl.
3. Pour dressing over vegetables and mix well.
4. Serve chill and enjoy!

NUTRITION:

327"calories", "protein"10 g, "carbohydrate" 23 g, "fats" 20 g

Tuna & veggies salad

Preparation time: 15 minutes | Cooking time: 15 minutes

Servings:2

INGREDIENTS

- 1 egg, boil cut into halves
- 1 cup tuna, steamed
- 1 avocado sliced
- 4-5 zucchini, sliced
- 4-5 lettuce leaves, chopped
- 4 oz. Green beans
- Salt and pepper to taste

DIRECTIONS

1. Add veggies, tuna and boiled egg in serving bowl.

2. Drizzle salt and pepper on top and mix it.
3. Serve and enjoy!

NUTRITION:

348"calories", "protein"22 g, "carbohydrate" 32 g, "fats" 18 g,

Falafel fresh salad

Preparation time: 10 minutes | Cooking time:20 minutes

Servings: 2

INGREDIENTS

- 4 medium zucchini, cut into thick slice
- Salt and pepper to taste
- 2 tortilla
- 4-5 falafel
- Lettuce leaves
- 1/4 cup Greek yogurt

DIRECTIONS

1. Toss tortilla on a griddle for about 2-3 minutes.
2. Arrange falafel, zucchini slice, lettuce leaves on tortilla and top with Greek yogurt.
3. Drizzle salt and pepper on top.
4. Serve and enjoy!

NUTRITION:

297"calories", "protein"12 g, "carbohydrate" 40 g, "fats" 9 g

Tacos with guacamole & chickpeas

Preparation time: 10 minutes | Cooking time:20 minutes

Servings: 2

INGREDIENTS

- 1 cup guacamole
- 4 zucchini, sliced
- 1 cup chickpeas, boiled
- 12–15 mint leaves, finely chopped
- Arugula leaves
- Salt & pepper
- 3–4 tbsps. Lime juice

DIRECTIONS

1. Spread guacamole in a plate with knife.
2. Arrange zucchini slice, chickpeas and arugula leaves on it.
3. Drizzle lime juice, salt, and pepper on top.
4. Serve and enjoy!

NUTRITION:

429"calories", "protein"15 g, "carbohydrate" 41 g, "fats" 18 g

★ ★ ★ ★ ★

Cucumber salad

Preparation time: 10 minutes | Cooking time:20 minutes

Servings: 2

INGREDIENTS

- 2 cucumbers, thinly sliced
- Salt & pepper
- 3–4 tbsps. Lime juice

DIRECTIONS

1. Add cucumber slice in serving plate.
2. Drizzle, lime juice, salt and pepper on top.
3. Serve chill and enjoy it!

NUTRITION:

60"calories", "protein"1 g, "carbohydrate" 13 g, "fats" 0 g

Cobb salad traditional

Preparation time: 20 minutes | Cooking time:10 minutes

Servings: 4

INGREDIENTS

- 1/3 cup lime juice
- 1 tbsp. Mustard
- Salt & pepper
- 1 bunch romaine lettuce, chopped
- 4 hard-boiled eggs, peeled and quartered
- 12 oz. Boil chicken, diced
- 1 avocado, thinly sliced
- 5 oz. Zucchini, halved

DIRECTIONS

1. Mix lime juice, mustard, salt, and pepper in jar.
2. Arrange vegetables in serving platter and top with dressing ingredients.
3. Season with salt and pepper, drizzle with dressing.
4. Serve and enjoy!

NUTRITION:

380"calories", "protein"30 g, "carbohydrate" 14 g, "fats" 18 g

★ ★ ★ ★ ★

Avocado salad

Preparation time: 10 minutes | Cooking time: minutes

Servings: 2

INGREDIENTS

- 1 avocado, thinly sliced
- 1 bunch lettuce leaves, chopped

DIRECTIONS

1. Add all ingredients in serving plate.
2. Serve and enjoy!

NUTRITION:

165"calories", "protein"2 g, "carbohydrate" 9 g, "fats" 14 g

★ ★ ★ ★ ★

Zucchini and Avocado Salad

Preparation Time: 10 minutes | Cooking Time: 0 minutes

Servings: 4

Ingredients:

- 1 lb. zucchini
- 2 avocados
- 1 and 1/2 tbsp olive oil
- Handful basil, chopped

Directions:

1. Mix the zucchini with the avocados and the rest of the ingredients in a serving bowl, toss and serve right away.

Nutrition:

Calories: 148 kcal; Protein: 5.5 g; Carbohydrates: 9 g; Fat: 7.8 g

★ ★ ★ ★ ★

Beans and Cucumber Salad

Preparation Time: 10 minutes | Cooking Time: 0 minutes

Servings: 4

Ingredients:

- 15 oz. great northern beans. canned
- 2 tbsp olive oil
- 1/2 cup baby arugula
- 1 cup cucumber
- 1 tbsp parsley
- 2 zucchini, cubed
- 2 tbsp balsamic vinegar

Directions:

1. Mix the beans with the cucumber and the rest of the ingredients in a large bowl, toss and serve cold.

Nutrition:

Calories: 233 kcal; Protein: 8 g; Carbohydrates: 13 g; Fat: 9 g

Chickpeas and quinoa salad

Preparation time: 10 minutes | Cooking time:25 minutes

Servings: 2

INGREDIENTS

- 1 cup chickpeas, boil

- 1 cup quinoa, cooked
- 4-5 zucchini, chopped
- 8 oz. Spinach, chopped
- Salt and pepper
- 3–4 tbsps. Lime juice

DIRECTIONS

1. Add all cooked items and chopped veggies in bowl and mix well.
2. Serve and enjoy!

NUTRITION:

347"calories", "protein"17 g, "carbohydrate" 64 g, "fats" 3 g

Beets and Honey Salad

Preparation time: 10 minutes | Cooking time: 7 hours

Servings: 12

INGREDIENTS:

- 5 beets, peeled and sliced
- 1/4 cup balsamic vinegar
- 1/3 cup honey
- 1 tablespoon rosemary, chopped
- 2 tablespoons olive oil

DIRECTIONS:

1. In your Slow cooker, mix beets with vinegar, honey, oil, and rosemary, cover, and cook on Low for 7 hours.
2. Divide between plates and serve as a side dish.

NUTRITION:

70 calories,0.8g protein, 12.3g carbohydrates, 2.5g fat, 1g fiber, 0mg

cholesterol, 33mg sodium, 140mg potassium.

Carrot Side Salad

Preparation time: 10 minutes | Cooking time: 7 hours

Servings: 6

INGREDIENTS:

- 1/2 cup walnuts, chopped
- 2 tablespoons olive oil
- 1 shallot, chopped
- 1 teaspoon Dijon mustard
- 1 tablespoon honey
- 2 beets, peeled and cut into wedges
- 2 carrots, peeled and sliced
- 1 cup parsley
- 5 ounces arugula

DIRECTIONS:

1. In your Slow cooker, mix beets with carrots, honey, mustard, shallot, oil, and walnuts, cover, and cook on Low for 7 hours.
2. Transfer everything to a bowl, add parsley and arugula, toss, divide between plates and serve as a side dish.

NUTRITION:

256 calories,4.3g protein, 11.3g carbohydrates, 12.4g fat, 2.7g fiber, 0mg cholesterol, 64mg sodium, 385mg potassium.

Arugula Salad

Preparation Time: 5 minutes | Cooking Time: 0 minutes

Servings: 4

Ingredients:

- 4 cup arugula leaves
- 1 cup zucchini
- 1/4 cup pine nuts
- 1 tbsp rice vinegar
- 2 tbsp olive/grapeseed oil
- 1/4 cup parmesan cheese, grated
- Black pepper and salt, as desired
- 1 large avocado, sliced

Directions:

1. Peel and slice the avocado. Rinse and dry the arugula leaves, grate the cheese, and slice the zucchini into halves.
2. Combine the arugula, pine nuts, zucchini, oil, vinegar, salt, pepper, and cheese.
3. Toss the salad to mix and portion it onto plates with the avocado slices to serve.

Nutrition:

Calories: 257 kcal; Protein: 6.1 g; Carbohydrates: 6 g; Fat: 5 g

★ ★ ★ ★ ★

Chopped Israeli Mediterranean Pasta Salad

Preparation Time: 15 minutes | Cooking Time: 2 minutes

Servings: 8

Ingredients:

- 1/2 lb. small bow tie or other small pasta
- 1/3 cup cucumber
- 1/3 cup radish
- 1/3 cup zucchini
- 1/3 cup yellow bell pepper
- 1/3 cup orange bell pepper
- 1/3 cup black olives
- 1/3 cup green olives
- 1/3 cup pepperoncini
- 1/3 cup feta cheese
- 1/3 cup fresh thyme leaves
- 1 tsp oregano, dried

Dressing:

- 1/4 cup + more, olive oil

Directions:

1. Slice the green olives into halves. Dice the feta and pepperoncini. Finely dice the remainder of the veggies.
2. Prepare a pot of water with the salt, and simmer the pasta until it's al dente (checking at 2 minutes under the listed time). Rinse and drain in cold water.
3. Combine a small amount of oil with the pasta. Add the salt, pepper, oregano, thyme, and veggies. Pour in the rest of the oil, mix and fold in the grated feta.
4. Pop it into the fridge within 2 hours, best if overnight. Taste test and adjust the seasonings to your liking; add fresh thyme.

Nutrition:

Calories: 65 kcal; Protein: 0.8 g; Carbohydrates: 6 g; Fat: 8 g

Feta Zucchini Salad

Preparation Time: 5 minutes | Cooking Time: 0 minutes

Servings: 4

Ingredients:

- 2 tbsp balsamic vinegar
- 1tsp basil, freshly minced, or .5 tsp, dried
- 0.5 tsp salt
- 2 tbsp olive oil
- 1 lb. zucchini
- 1/4 cup low-fat feta cheese, crumbled

Directions:

1. Whisk the salt, basil, and vinegar.
2. Slice the zucchini into halves and stir in the feta cheese, and oil to serve.

Nutrition:

Calories: 121 kcal; Protein: 3 g; Carbohydrates: 10 g; Fat: 6 g

Tofu Salad

Preparation Time: 10 minutes | Cooking Time: 15 minutes

Servings: 2

Ingredients:

- 1/2 pack firm tofu

- 2 spelt tortillas
- 1 avocado
- 4 handfuls baby spinach
- 1 handful almonds
- 2 zucchini
- 1 pink grapefruit

Directions:

1. Heat the tortillas in an oven and once warm, bake for 8–10 minutes in the oven.
2. Chop up the zucchini, and tofu and combine this. Put it in the fridge and let it cool.
3. Now chop up the almonds, avocado, and grapefruit. Mix everything well and place nicely around the bowl you had put in the fridge.
4. Enjoy!

Nutrition:

Calories: 110 kcal; Protein: 36 g; Carbohydrates: 19 g; Fat: 11 g

★ ★ ★ ★ ★

Minty Olives and Zucchini Salad

Preparation Time: 10 minutes | Cooking Time: 0 minutes

Servings: 4

Ingredients:

- 1 cup Kalamata olives
- 1 cup black olives
- 1 cup zucchini
- 4 zucchini
- 2 tbsp oregano, chopped
- 1 tbsp mint, chopped

- 2 tbsp balsamic vinegar
- 1/4 cup olive oil
- 2 tsp Italian herbs, dried

Directions:

1. In a salad bowl, mix the olives with the zucchini and the rest of the ingredients, toss, and serve cold.

Nutrition:

Calories: 190 kcal; Protein: 4.6 g; Carbohydrates: 9 g; Fat: 8.1 g

Persimmon Salad

Preparation Time: 10 minutes | Cooking Time: 0 minutes

Servings: 4

Ingredients:

- Seeds from 1 pomegranate
- 2 persimmons, cored and sliced
- 5 cups baby arugula
- 4 navel oranges, cut into segments
- 1/4 cup white vinegar
- 1/3 cup olive oil
- 3 tbsp pine nuts
- 1 and 1/2 tsp orange zest, grated
- 2 tbsp orange juice
- 1 tbsp coconut sugar
- 1/2 shallot, chopped
- A pinch of cinnamon powder

Directions:

1. In a salad bowl, combine the pomegranate seeds with

persimmons, arugula, and oranges, and toss. In another bowl, combine the vinegar with the oil, pine nuts, orange zest, orange juice, coconut sugar, shallot, and cinnamon, whisk well, add to the salad, toss and serve as a side dish.

Nutrition:

Calories: 310 kcal; Protein: 7 g; Carbohydrates: 33 g; Fat: 16 g

★ ★ ★ ★ ★

Olives and Lentils Salad

Preparation Time: 10 minutes | Cooking Time: 0 minutes

Servings: 2

Ingredients:

- 1/3 cup green lentils canned
- 1 tbsp olive oil
- 2 cups baby spinach
- 1 cup black olives
- 2 tbsp sunflower seeds
- 1 tbsp Dijon mustard
- 2 tbsp balsamic vinegar
- 2 tbsp olive oil

Directions:

1. Mix the lentils with the spinach, olives, and the rest of the ingredients in a salad bowl, toss and serve cold.

Nutrition:

Calories: 279 kcal; Protein: 12 g; Carbohydrates: 6.9 g; Fat: 5.5 g

★ ★ ★ ★ ★

Avocado Side Salad

Preparation Time: 10 minutes | Cooking Time: 0 minutes

Servings: 4

Ingredients:

- 4 blood oranges, slice into segments
- 2 tbsp olive oil
- A pinch of red pepper, crushed
- 2 avocados, peeled, cut into wedges
- 1 and 1/2 cups baby arugula

Directions:

1. Mix the oranges with the oil, red pepper, avocados, arugula, and almonds in a bowl, and then serve.

Nutrition:

Calories: 146 kcal; Protein: 15 g; Carbohydrates: 8 g; Fat: 7 g

★ ★ ★ ★ ★

Broccoli Salad

Preparation Time: 15 minutes| Cooking Time: 20 minutes

Servings: 4

Ingredients:

For the Salad:

- Kosher salt
- 3 broccoli heads
- 1/4 cup almond, toasted
- 2 tbsp fresh chives

For the dressing:

- 1 tbsp mayonnaise

- 3 tbsp apple cider
- 1 tbsp Dijon mustard
- Kosher salt
- Black paper, ground

Directions:

1. Heat 6 cups of salted water in a medium pot. Then prepare a large bowl with ice water. Mix in the broccoli florets and cook until tender. Take it out from the pan, then transfer it to the bowl with ice water. When it cools down, drain the broccoli.

2. Whisk all the dressing ingredients and season it well to your desired taste. Then mix all the salad ingredients in a separate bowl and pour the dressing. Toss it well until fully coated. Let it chill before serving.

Nutrition:

Calories: 150 kcal; Protein: 19 g; Carbohydrates: 5 g; Fat: 2 g

★ ★ ★ ★ ★

Tabbouleh Salad

Preparation Time: 20 minutes | Cooking Time: 15 minutes

Servings: 4

Ingredients:

- 2 cups water, filtered
- 1 cup millet, rinsed
- 1/3 cup extra-virgin olive oil
- 1 1/2 tsp Himalayan pink salt, divided
- 2 large zucchini, rinsed and finely diced
- 3 scallions, white parts only, rinsed and thinly sliced
- 1/2 English cucumber, rinsed and finely diced
- 3/4 cup fresh mint, rinsed and finely chopped
- 1 1/2 cup fresh parsley, rinsed and finely chopped

Directions:

1. Boil water over high heat. Add the millet and turn the heat to low. Cover the pan and cook for 15 minutes.
2. Remove the pan from the heat and mash the millet with a fork. Let cool with the lid off for 15 minutes. It should be firm but not crunchy or mushy.
3. Meanwhile, in a small bowl, whisk the olive oil, and ½ tsp of salt. Let sit.
4. In a large bowl, combine the zucchini, scallions, cucumber, mint, and parsley. Add the cooled millet. Pour the dressing over and mix well. Taste and season with the remaining 1 tsp of salt, as needed.

Nutrition:

Calories: 360 kcal; Protein: 8 g; Carbohydrates: 44 g; Fat: 20 g

Guacamole Salad

Preparation Time: 10 minutes | Cooking Time: 0 minute

Servings: 2

Ingredients:

- 2 avocados, halved and pitted
- 1/2 cup fresh cilantro, rinsed and chopped
- Juice of 1/2 lime
- 1 slice jalapeño
- 1/2 tsp Himalayan pink salt
- 1 zucchini, rinsed and diced

Directions:

1. Take the avocado flesh into a medium bowl. Stir in the cilantro, lime juice, cayenne, and salt. Mash everything until

smooth.

2. Add the zucchini, mix well, and serve.

Nutrition:

Calories: 450 kcal; Protein: 5 g; Carbohydrates: 27 g; Fat: 30 g

★ ★ ★ ★ ★

Buckwheat Salad

Preparation Time: 10 minutes | Cooking Time: 15 minutes

Servings: 2

Ingredients:

- 1 cup raw buckwheat, rinsed
- 2 cup water
- 2 handfuls fresh baby spinach leaves, rinsed
- Handful fresh basil leaves, rinsed
- 2 scallions, white parts only, rinsed and chopped
- Himalayan pink salt
- Black pepper, freshly ground
- 1/4 cup extra-virgin olive oil
- 2 tbsp mixed sprouts, rinsed
- 1 ripe avocado, peeled, pitted, and sliced
- 1 1/2 oz. low-fat feta cheese (optional)

Directions:

1. Mix the buckwheat and water, then bring it to a boil over high heat. Reduce the heat to simmer and cook for 15 minutes, or until soft. Remove from the heat and let cool.
2. Meanwhile, in a food processor, combine the baby spinach, basil, scallions, and process for 30 seconds. Stir the herb mixture into the cooled buckwheat.
3. Arrange the buckwheat on a platter. Drizzle with the olive oil.

Top with the sliced avocado, crumble the feta over top (if using), and serve.

Nutrition:

Calories: 385 kcal; Protein: 6 g; Carbohydrates: 43 g; Fat: 24 g

★ ★ ★ ★ ★

Mixed Sprouts Salad

Preparation Time: 10 minutes | Cooking Time: 0 minute

Servings: 2

Ingredients:

- 1–2 tbsp coconut oil
- Handful fresh chives, rinsed and chopped
- Handful fresh dill, rinsed and chopped
- Handful fresh parsley, rinsed and chopped
- 1/2 tsp Himalayan pink salt
- 1/2 tsp black pepper, freshly ground
- 1 scallion, rinsed and chopped
- 1 cucumber, rinsed and chopped
- 1/2 cup mixed sprouts of choice (alfalfa, radish, broccoli, mung bean, cress, etc.), rinsed

Directions:

1. In a blender, combine the coconut oil, chives, dill, parsley, salt, and pepper, and blend until mainly smooth.
2. Transfer to a medium bowl. Stir in the scallion, cucumber, and sprouts to coat, and serve.

Nutrition:

Calories: 168 kcal; Protein: 5 g; Carbohydrates: 12 g; Fat: 14 g

★ ★ ★ ★ ★

Sweet Potato Salad

Preparation Time: 15 minutes | Cooking Time: 5 minutes

Servings: 2

Ingredients:

For the dressing:

- 1/2 cup sesame oil
- 2 tbsp coconut oil
- 2 tbsp light soy sauce
- 1 tbsp coconut sugar or raw honey

For the salad:

- 5 1/2 oz. fresh baby spinach leaves, rinsed
- 1 zucchini, chopped
- 1 tbsp coconut oil
- 1 large sweet potato, scrubbed, peeled, and diced

Directions:

To make the dressing:

1. In a small bowl, whisk the sesame oil, coconut oil, soy sauce, and coconut sugar until blended. Set aside.

To make the salad:

1. In a large salad bowl, gently toss together the baby spinach, and zucchini. Set aside.
2. In a small skillet over medium heat, heat the coconut oil. Add the sweet potato and cook for 3–5 minutes, stirring, until golden brown. Using a slotted spoon, add the sweet potato to the salad and gently stir to combine. Pour the dressing over the salad, gently toss again to coat, and serve.

Nutrition:

Calories: 150 kcal; Protein: 8 g; Carbohydrates: 20 g; Fat: 12 g

★ ★ ★ ★ ★

Waldorf Salad

Preparation Time: 15 minutes plus overnight to soak

Cooking Time: 0 minute | Servings: 2

Ingredients:

For the dressing:

- 1 ripe avocado, peeled and pitted
- 1 tsp Dijon mustard
- 1/2 tsp Himalayan pink salt
- Black pepper, freshly ground

For the salad:

- 2 cup chickpeas, canned, rinsed and drained, or cooked, drained, and cooled
- 1 cup sunflower seeds, soaked in filtered water overnight, drained
- 2 apples, rinsed, cored, and chopped
- 1 celery stalk, rinsed and diced
- 1–2 tsp fresh dill, chopped and rinsed

Directions:

To make the dressing:

1. In a small bowl, using a fork, mash together the avocado, mustard, salt, pepper. Set aside

To make the salad:

1. In a large bowl, stir together the chickpeas, sunflower seeds, and dressing until well combined. Stir in the apples and celery. Top with the fresh dill and serve.

Nutrition:

Calories: 700 kcal; Protein: 6 g; Carbohydrates: 22 g; Fat: 10 g

★ ★ ★ ★ ★

Radish and Olives Salad

Preparation Time: 5 minutes | Cooking Time: 0 minutes

Servings: 4

Ingredients:

- 1 lb. radishes, cubed
- 2 tbsp balsamic vinegar
- 2 tbsp olive oil
- 1 cup black olives, pitted and halved
- A pinch black pepper

Directions:

1. Mix radishes with the other ingredients in a large salad bowl, toss, and serve as a side dish.

Nutrition:

Calories: 123 kcal; Protein: 1.3 g; Carbohydrates: 6.9 g; Fat: 10.8 g

★ ★ ★ ★ ★

Vegetable and Sides

Basil Olives Mix

Preparation Time: 5 minutes | Cooking Time: 0 minutes

Servings: 4

Ingredients:

- 2 tbsp olive oil
- 1 tbsp balsamic vinegar
- A pinch black pepper
- 4 cups corn
- 2 cups black olives, pitted and halved
- 1/2 cup zucchini, halved
- 1 tbsp basil, chopped
- 1 tbsp jalapeno, chopped
- 2 cups romaine lettuce, shredded

Directions:

1. Mix the corn with the olives, lettuce, and the other ingredients in a large bowl, toss well, divide between plates and have it as a side dish.

Nutrition:

Calories: 290 kcal; Protein: 6.2 g; Carbohydrates: 37.6 g; Fat: 16.1 g

★ ★ ★ ★ ★

Artichoke and Kale Stuffed Mushrooms

Preparation Time: 15 minutes | Cooking Time: 28 minutes

Servings: 4

Ingredients:

- 16 large white button mushrooms, stemmed
- 2 tsp olive oil

- 1 cup water-packed artichoke hearts, canned and chopped
- 2 cups kale, finely shredded
- 1 tsp fresh basil, chopped
- 1 tsp fresh oregano, chopped
- 1/8 tsp sea salt

Directions:

1. Preheat the oven to 375°F (190°C).
2. On a baking sheet, hollow-side up to arrange the mushroom caps.
3. Heat the olive oil in a large skillet over medium-high heat.
4. Add the artichoke hearts, kale, basil, oregano, and sea salt. Sauté until the kale is wilted, about 5 minutes.
5. Squeeze the liquid out of the filling into the skillet with the back of a spoon and divide the mixture evenly among the mushroom caps.
6. Bake until the mushrooms are tender, about 20 minutes. Serve warm.

Nutrition:

Calories: 75 kcal; Protein: 5 g; Fat: 3 g; Carbohydrates: 11 g

Zucchini Bulgur

Preparation Time: 7 minutes | Cooking Time: 20 minutes

Servings: 2

Ingredients:

- 1/2 cup bulgur
- 1 tsp zucchini paste
- 2 tbsp coconut oil
- 1 1/2 cup chicken stock

Directions:

1. Toss coconut oil in the pan and melt it.
2. Then add bulgur and stir well.
3. Cook bulgur in coconut oil for 3 minutes.
4. Then add zucchini paste and mix up bulgur until homogenous.
5. Add chicken stock.
6. Close the lid and cook bulgur for 15 minutes over the medium heat.
7. The cooked bulgur should soak all liquid.

Nutrition:

Calories: 257 kcal; Protein: 5.2 g; Carbohydrates: 30.2 g; Fat: 14.5 g

Roasted Butternut Squash with Apples

Preparation Time: 10 minutes | Cooking Time: 20 minutes

Portions: 4

INGREDIENTS:

- 2 tbsp oliva oil
- 1 tbsp cinnamon
- 1 butternut squash peeled, seeded, cubes
- 3 medium apples peeled, cubes

DIRECTION:

1. Preheat oven to 400 degrees Fahrenheit. Coat a large, rimmed baking sheet with cooking spray before lining it with foil. In a single layer, arrange the squash and apples. Over the top, drizzle the oil and toss to coat. Cinnamon should be sprinkled on top.
2. Bake for 25 minutes in a preheated oven, stirring once or twice during that time. If preferred, top with more cinnamon and

serve right away!

NUTRITION:

Calories: 175 Total Fat: 8g Total Carbohydrates: 28g Protein: 2g

★ ★ ★ ★ ★

Moroccan Style Couscous

Preparation Time: 10 minutes | Cooking Time: 10 minutes

Servings: 4

Ingredients:

- 1/2 tsp cardamom, ground
- 1 cup chicken stock
- 1 tbsp butter
- 1 tsp salt
- 1/2 tsp red pepper

Directions:

1. Toss butter in the pan and melt it.
2. Add couscous and roast it for 1 minute over the high heat.
3. Then add ground cardamom, salt, and red pepper. Stir it well.
4. Pour the chicken stock and bring the mixture to boil.
5. Simmer couscous for 5 minutes with the closed lid.

Nutrition:

Calories: 196 kcal; Protein: 5.9 g; Carbohydrates: 35 g; Fat: 3.4 g

★ ★ ★ ★ ★

Roasted Curried Cauliflower

Preparation Time: 5 minutes | Cooking Time: 30 minutes

Servings: 4

Ingredients:

- 1 large head cauliflower, cut into florets
- 1 and 1/2 tbsp olive oil
- 1 tsp cumin seeds
- 1 tsp mustard seeds
- 3/4 tsp salt

Directions:

1. Preheat your oven to 375°F.
2. Grease a baking sheet with cooking spray.
3. Take a bowl and place all ingredients.
4. Toss to coat well.
5. Arrange the vegetable on a baking sheet.
6. Roast for 30 minutes.
7. Serve and enjoy!

Nutrition:

Calories: 67 kcal; Protein: 2 g; Carbohydrates: 4 g; Fat: 6 g

Caramelized Pears

Preparation Time: 5 minutes | Cooking Time: 35 minutes

Servings: 4

Ingredients:

- 2 firm red pears, cored and quartered
- 1 tbsp olive oil
- Salt and pepper, to taste

Directions:

1. Preheat your oven to 425°F.
2. Place the pears on a baking tray.
3. Drizzle with olive oil.
4. Season with salt and pepper.
5. Bake in the oven for 35 minutes.
6. Serve and enjoy!

Nutrition:

Calories: 101 kcal; Protein: 1 g; Carbohydrates: 17 g; Fat: 4 g

Ethiopian Cabbage Delight

Preparation Time: 15 minutes | Cooking Time: 6–8 hours

Servings: 6

Ingredients:

- 1/2 cup water
- 1 head green cabbage, cored and chopped
- 1 lb. sweet potatoes, peeled and chopped
- 3 carrots, peeled and chopped
- 1 tsp extra virgin olive oil
- 1/2 tsp turmeric, ground
- 1/2 tsp cumin, ground
- 1/4 tsp ginger, ground

Directions:

1. Add water to your Slow Cooker.
2. Take a medium bowl and add cabbage, carrots, sweet potatoes, and mix.
3. Add olive oil, turmeric, ginger, cumin and toss until the veggies are fully coated.

4. Transfer veggie mix to your Slow Cooker.

5. Cover and cook on LOW for 6–8 hours.

6. Serve and enjoy!

Nutrition:

Calories: 155 kcal; Protein: 4 g; Carbohydrates: 35 g; Fat: 2 g

★ ★ ★ ★ ★

Cool Garbanzo and Spinach Beans

Preparation Time: 5–10 minutes | Cooking Time: 0 minute

Servings: 4

Ingredients:

- 12 oz. garbanzo beans
- 1 tbsp olive oil
- 1/2 tsp cumin
- 10 oz. spinach, chopped

Directions:

1. Take a skillet and add olive oil.

2. Place it over medium-low heat.

3. Add garbanzo and cook for 5 minutes.

4. Stir in cumin, garbanzo beans, spinach and season with sunflower seeds.

5. Use a spoon to smash gently.

6. Cook thoroughly.

7. Serve and enjoy!

Nutrition:

Calories: 90 kcal; Protein: 4 g; Carbohydrates: 11 g; Fat: 4 g

★ ★ ★ ★ ★

Avocado Cucumber Sushi

Preparation Time: 20 minutes | Cooking Time: 15 minutes

Servings: 4

Ingredients:

- 1 1/2 cups dry quinoa
- 6 nori sheets
- 3 avocados, halved, pitted, and sliced thin, divided
- 1 small cucumber, halved, seeded, and cut into matchsticks, divided
- 3 cups water, plus additional for rolling
- 1/2 tsp salt
- Coconut aminos, for dipping (optional)

Directions:

1. In a fine-mesh sieve, rinse the quinoa.
2. Add the rinsed quinoa, water, and salt into a medium pot, bring to a boil over high heat. Reduce the heat to low. Cover and simmer for 15 minutes. Use a fork to fluff the quinoa.
3. Lay out 1 nori sheet on a cutting board, spread ½ cup of quinoa over the sheet, leaving 2 to 3 inches uncovered at the top.
4. Put 5 or 6 avocado slices across the bottom of the nori sheet in a row. Add 5 or 6 cucumber matchsticks on top.
5. From the bottom, roll up the nori sheet tightly. Dab the uncovered top with water to seal the roll.
6. Cut the sushi roll into 6 pieces.
7. Repeat with the remaining 5 nori sheets, quinoa, and vegetables.
8. After all is done, serve the sushi with the coconut aminos (if using).

Nutrition:

Calories: 240 kcal; Protein: 8 g; Carbohydrates: 18 g; Fat: 6 g

☆ ☆ ☆ ☆ ☆

Kale, Mushroom, Walnut, and Avocado

Preparation Time: 10 minutes | Cooking Time: 15 minutes

Servings: 2–3

Ingredients:

- 6 kale leaves, chopped
- 10 walnuts, crushed
- 1/4 red bell pepper, diced
- 1/2 zucchini, sliced
- 20 mushrooms, sliced
- 1/2–1 tbsp avocado oil

Dressing:

- 1 tbsp key lime juice
- 1 tbsp sesame oil
- 1 zucchini
- 1/8 tsp sea salt
- 1/4 avocado

Directions:

Dressing:

1. Blend the lime juice, sesame oil, zucchini, salt, and avocado together until smooth. Sauté the mushrooms in the avocado oil.
2. Let cool afterward. Mix the kale, walnuts, pepper, zucchini, and mushrooms together.
3. Pour the dressing into the salad, then toss it well until it evenly coats the entire salad.

Nutrition:

Calories: 87 kcal; Protein: 10 g; Carbohydrates: 22 g; Fat: 1 g

★ ★ ★ ★ ★

Mix-Mix Alkaline Veggie

Preparation Time: 5 minutes | Cooking Time: 10 minutes

Servings: 2

Ingredients:

- 15 kale leaves, chopped
- 1 cup watercress leaves
- 1 cucumber, diced
- 2 tbsp fresh dill, finely chopped
- 5–10 olives, sliced
- 1/4 red bell pepper, chopped
- 1/4 green bell pepper, chopped
- 1 tbsp 100% date sugar syrup
- 3 tbsp water
- 1/8 tsp sea salt

Directions:

1. Mix the date sugar syrup, water, and salt together. Stir the remaining ingredients together in a bowl. Massage in date syrup mix with the vegetables.
2. Toss and serve.

Nutrition:

Calories: 102 kcal; Protein: 3 g; Carbohydrates: 6 g; Fat: 3 g

★ ★ ★ ★ ★

Seasoned Wild Rice

Preparation Time: 5 minutes | Cooking Time: 25 minutes

Servings: 1–2

Ingredients:

- 1 cup wild rice (soak wild rice overnight)
- 2–3 cup water (3 cup water if you didn't soak the rice overnight)
- 1 tbsp coconut oil
- 2 tsp oregano
- 1/2 tsp sea salt
- 2–3 scallions, chopped
- 1 zucchini, chopped

Directions:

1. Soaking the rice in water overnight reduces the cooking time for the rice.
2. Transfer all the ingredients to a saucepan over high heat and let them come to a boil.
3. Cover the saucepan and reduce to a simmer and allow the water to absorb into the rice. If you soaked the rice overnight, cook the rice for 25 minutes.
4. If you did not soak the rice overnight, cook for 50–60 minutes.

Nutrition:

Calories: 220 kcal; Protein: 5 g; Carbohydrates: 26 g; Fat: 4 g

★ ★ ★ ★ ★

Simply Chayote Squash

Preparation Time: 10 minutes | Cooking Time: 20 minutes

Servings: 1

Ingredients:

- 1 chayote squash
- 1/4 tsp coconut oil
- Dash cayenne pepper
- Dash sea salt

Directions:

1. Wash and cut chayote squash in half. The seed can be eaten, and it has a nice texture. Add chayote, oil, and enough water to cover the chayote in a saucepan.
2. Boil for 20 minutes until the fork can penetrate the squash, but the squash should still maintain some firmness. Remove from water. Season it well with cayenne pepper and salt.
3. Serve as a light snack or part of a dish.

Nutrition:

Calories: 117 kcal; Protein: 4 g; Carbohydrates: 12 g; Fat: 6 g

★ ★ ★ ★ ★

Vegetable Medley Sauté

Preparation Time: 10 minutes | Cooking Time: 15 minutes

Servings: 4

Ingredients:

- 1 cup mushrooms, sliced
- 1 zucchini, sliced
- 1 yellow squash, sliced
- 1 red pepper, chopped

- 1 green pepper, chopped
- 2 zucchini, chopped
- 1/2 cup chayote, finely chopped
- 3 tbsp grape-seed oil or avocado oil
- 1/8 tsp cayenne pepper
- 1/8 tsp sea salt

Directions:

1. Cook the oil in a saucepan over medium heat. Let the oil get hot.
2. Add in mushrooms and sauté for 4 minutes. Add in the rest of the vegetables and spices and sauté for 8–10 minutes.

Nutrition:

Calories: 115 kcal; Protein: 11 g; Carbohydrates: 20 g; Fat: 6 g

Desserts

Apple Couscous Pudding

Preparation Time: 10 minutes | Cooking Time: 25 minutes

Servings: 4

Ingredients:

- 1/2 cup couscous
- 1/2 cups milk
- 1/4 cup apple, cored and chopped
- 2 tbsp stevia
- 1/2 tsp rose water
- 1 tbsp orange zest, grated

Directions:

1. Heat a pan with the milk over medium heat, add the couscous and the rest of the ingredients, whisk, simmer for 25 minutes, divide into bowls and serve.

Nutrition:

Calories: 150 kcal; Protein: 4 g; Carbohydrates: 7.5 g; Fat: 4.5 g

Rice Pudding

Preparation Time: 5 minutes | Cooking Time: 20 minutes

Servings: 4

Ingredients:

- 4 1/3 cup almond milk, unsweetened
- 3 1/2 oz. brown rice
- 1 tbsp brown sugar, packed
- 2 tbsp pure maple syrup, separated

Directions:

1. Empty milk in a saucepan on the highest heat setting. As it

starts to bubble, turn the heat to medium/low, then transfer the rice into the pot.

2. Toss to cover the rice completely. Blend sugar and integrate fully. Toss frequently for 20 minutes or until it reaches the desired thickness.

3. Transfer to serving dishes and drizzle with ½ tbsp each with maple syrup.

Nutrition:

Calories: 100 kcal; Protein: 6 g; Carbohydrates: 22 g; Fat: 3 g

★ ★ ★ ★ ★

Pudding Glass with Banana and Whipped Cream

Preparation Time: 10 minutes | Cooking Time: 8 minutes

Servings: 2

Ingredients:

- 2 portions banana cream pudding mix
- 2 1/2 cups rice milk
- 8 oz. soy whipped cream
- 12 oz. vanilla wafers

Directions:

1. Put vanilla wafers in a pan, and in another bowl, mix banana cream pudding and rice milk.
2. Boil the ingredients, blending them slowly.
3. Pour the mixture over the wafers and make 2 or 3 layers.
4. Put the pan in the fridge for one hour and afterward spread the whipped topping over the dessert.
5. Put it back in the fridge for 2 hours and serve it cold in transparent glasses. Serve and enjoy!

Nutrition:

Calories: 255 kcal; Protein: 3 g; Carbohydrates: 13 g; Fat: 8 g

Carrot Cake Bites

Preparation Time: 10 minutes | Cooking Time: 0 minutes

Servings: 4

Ingredients:

- 4 baby carrots, peeled and chopped
- 1/8 tsp pure vanilla extract, sugar-free
- 1/3 cup coconut, shredded and unsweetened
- 2 tbsp almond butter, unsalted
- 1/8 tsp cinnamon, ground
- 1 tbsp pure maple syrup
- 1/3 cup gluten-free oats, rolled
- 1/8 tsp salt, iodized

Directions:

1. Thoroughly clean carrots and remove the skins. Chop into big chunks and transfer to a food blender.
2. Pulse for approximately 2 minutes until consistency is slightly chunky. Transfer to a glass dish.
3. Combine coconut and oats in a food blender and pulse for an additional 2 minutes.
4. Empty carrots, almond butter, maple syrup, salt, vanilla extract, and cinnamon in a food blender and pulse for a total of 2 minutes until the batter thickens. Section into 4 pieces and hand roll into spheres.
5. Serve immediately and enjoy!

Nutrition:

Calories: 160 kcal; Protein: 9 g; Carbohydrates: 12 g; Fat: 4 g

★ ★ ★ ★ ★

Pumpkin Peanut Pudding

Preparation Time: 10 minutes | Cooking Time: 0 minutes

Servings: 4

Ingredients:

- 1/8 tsp nutmeg, ground
- 1/2 cup peanuts, raw and unsalted
- 1/8 tsp salt, iodized
- 1/3 cup pumpkin puree
- 1/4 tsp cinnamon, ground
- 1/8 cup pure maple syrup
- 1/4 cup almond milk, unsweetened
- 1/2 tbsp coconut oil, melted
- 1/8 cloves, ground

Directions:

1. Pulse nutmeg, peanuts, salt, pumpkin puree, cinnamon, maple syrup, almond milk, coconut oil, and cloves for approximately 3 minutes.
2. Make sure all ingredients are incorporated. Divide equally into individual glasses or a dish.
3. Serve immediately and enjoy!

Nutrition:

Calories: 140 kcal; Protein: 2 g; Carbohydrates: 18 g; Fat: 5 g

★ ★ ★ ★ ★

Berry Blast

Preparation Time: 15 minutes | Cooking Time: 40 minutes

Servings: 1

Ingredients:

- 4 cups blueberries (2 cups fresh and 2 cups frozen)
- 1 cup rolled oats
- 1 tsp cinnamon
- 2 tbsp all-purpose flour
- 2 tsp olive oil
- 1 tbsp maple syrup

Directions:

1. Coat a pie pan with cooking spray and set it aside. Put the blueberries on the pie plate. Preheat the oven to 250°F.
2. Combine the flour, oil, oats, maple syrup, and cinnamon in a large mixing bowl and whisk until you obtain a grainy mixture.
3. Transfer the oats mixture to the pie pan and bake for 40 minutes until the mixture is golden brown. Serve warm.

Nutrition:

Calories: 424 kcal; Fat: 10.2 g; Carbohydrates: 66.6 g; Protein: 4.9 g

★ ★ ★ ★ ★

Oats and Fruit Bar Cracker

Preparation Time: 15 minutes | Cooking Time: 0 minutes

Servings: 3

Ingredients:

- 1 cup quinoa
- 1 cup oats

- 1/2 cup figs, dried
- 1/2 cup honey
- 1/2 cup almonds, chopped
- 1/2 cup apricots, dried
- 1/2 cup wheat germ
- 1/2 cup pineapple, dried and chopped
- 1 tbsp cornstarch

Directions:

1. Mix the fixing in a mixing bowl until you obtain a well-balanced mixture. Put the batter on a baking tray or plate and flatten it. Ensure that the mixture is at least one inch thick. Let it cool before you cut it into pieces and serve.

Nutrition:

Calories: 296 kcal; Fat: 3.7 g; Carbohydrates: 144.2 g; Protein: 5.2 g

Colorful Pops

Preparation Time: 15 minutes | Cooking Time: 0 minutes

Servings: 6

Ingredients:

- 2 cups watermelon, strawberries, and cantaloupe, diced
- 2 cups pure apple juice
- 2 cups fresh blueberries
- 6 craft sticks
- 6 paper cups

Directions:

1. Mix all the fruit in a mixing bowl. Divide the fruit salad into the paper cups and pour the apple juice. Ensure that the apple juice only covers half the paper cup. Deep-freeze the cups for

an hour or until they are partially frozen.

2. Remove the cups and add the sticks to the cups, and deep freeze for 1 more hour. Serve them as colorful pops!

Nutrition:

Calories: 83 kcal; Fat: 0.2 g; Carbohydrates: 20.8 g; Protein: 0.7 g

★ ★ ★ ★ ★

Pumpkin Pie

Preparation Time: 15 minutes | Cooking Time: 50 minutes

Servings: 2

Ingredients:

- 1 cup ginger snaps
- 8 oz. pumpkin, canned
- 1/4 cup egg whites
- 1/4 cup raw brown sugar
- 1 tsp pumpkin pie spice
- 6 oz. skim milk, evaporated
- Cooking spray

Directions:

1. Preheat the oven to 300°F. Oiled a glass pie pan with cooking spray. Crumble the ginger snaps and pat them into the glass pan. Mix the rest of the fixing in a mixing bowl and pour it into the prepared glass pie pan.
2. Bake the dish for fifty minutes or until a knife inserted in the center comes out clean.
3. Transfer the pie pan to the refrigerator and allow it to cool. Serve cold.

Nutrition:

Calories: 392 kcal; Fat: 16.6 g; Carbohydrates: 80.7 g; Protein: 20 g

★ ★ ★ ★ ★

Walnut and Oatmeal Chocolate Chip Cookies

Preparation Time: 15 minutes | Cooking Time: 20 minutes

Servings: 4

Ingredients:

- 1 cup rolled oats
- 1/4 cup all-purpose flour
- 1/4 cup whole-wheat pastry flour
- 1/2 tsp cinnamon, ground
- 1/4 tsp baking soda
- 1/4 tsp salt
- 1/4 tsp tahini
- 2 tbsp olive oil
- 1/2 cup raw brown sugar
- 1/2 cup maple syrup
- 2 eggs (1 whole and 1 egg white)
- 1/2 tbsp vanilla extract
- 1/2 cup bittersweet chocolate chips
- 1/4 cup walnuts, chopped

Directions:

1. Place racks in the oven's upper and lower parts and preheat the oven to 300°F. Prepare or arrange two lined baking sheets with parchment paper. Combine the oats, whole-wheat flour, all-purpose flour, baking soda, cinnamon, and salt in a bowl and whisk.

2. Beat oil and tahini in a large mixing bowl and blend until you obtain a paste. Add maple syrup and erythritol to the bowl and continue to beat until you get a well-combined mixture. Note

that the mixture will still be slightly grainy.

3. Now, add the vanilla extract, egg white, and whole egg to the bowl and continue to whisk until you obtain a well-combined mixture.

4. Stir in the oat mixture, chocolate chips, and walnuts into the bowl. Wet your hands slightly, roll 1 tbsp of the batter into a small ball, and place it on the baking sheet. Flatten the ball out but ensure that the sides do not crack. Continue with the remaining batter and leave at least a 2-inch space between each cookie.

5. Bake the cookies for 20 minutes or until golden brown. Cool the cookies for 2 minutes before you transfer them onto the wire rack to cool completely.

Nutrition:

Calories: 530 kcal; Fat: 14.8 g; Carbohydrates: 98.6 g; Protein: 10.6 g

Apple Dumplings

Preparation Time: 10 minutes | Cooking Time: 30 minutes

Servings: 6

Ingredients:

Dough:

- 1 tbsp olive oil
- 1 tsp honey
- 1 cup whole-wheat flour
- 2 tbsp buckwheat flour
- 2 tbsp rolled oats

Apple filling:

- 6 large tart apples, thinly sliced

- 1 tsp nutmeg
- tbsp honey

Directions:

1. Warm oven to heat at 350°F. Combine flours with oats, honey, and oil in a food processor. Pulse this mixture for few times, then mix until it forms a ball. Wrap it in a plastic sheet.
2. Refrigerate for 2 hours. Mix apples with honey, and nutmeg, then set it aside. Spread the dough into ¼ inch thick sheet. Cut it into 8–inch circles and layer the greased muffin cups with the dough circles.
3. Divide the apple mixture into the muffin cups and seal the dough from the top. Bake for 30 minutes at 350°F until golden brown. Enjoy.

Nutrition:

Calories: 178 kcal; Fat: 5.7 g; Carbs: 32.4 g; Protein: 2.1 g

Banana Delight

Preparation Time: 15 minutes | Cooking Time: 12 minutes

Servings: 4

Ingredients:

- 1 tbsp sodium-free baking powder
- 1 tbsp raw brown sugar
- 1 cup flour
- 1 tbsp oil
- 1/4 cup egg substitute
- 1/2 tsp nutmeg
- 1 cup banana, chopped
- 1/2 cup soy milk

Directions:

1. In a bowl, mix and stir baking powder, sugar, and flour. Mix oil, egg, and milk, then add nutmeg and banana in a separate bowl. Add the mixture into the bowl of dry ingredients.

2. In a hot frying pan, drop just by tablespoonfuls and fry for about 2 to 3 minutes. Wait until it is golden brown, then drain and serve.

Nutrition:

Calories: 210.1 kcal; Protein: 5.7 g; Carbs: 37.6 g; Fat: 7.1 g

★ ★ ★ ★ ★

Healthy Banana-Choco Ice Cream

Preparation Time: 10 minutes | Cooking Time: 0 minutes

Servings: 4

Ingredients:

- 3 medium bananas, peeled and frozen
- 3 tbsp cocoa powder, unsweetened

Directions:

1. Place all the fixing in a blender and puree until it resembles soft-serve ice cream. Evenly divide into 4 bowls. Serve and enjoy

Nutrition:

Calories: 88 kcal; Protein: 1.7 g; Carbs: 22.6 g; Fat: 0.8 g

★ ★ ★ ★ ★

Healthy Chocolate Mousse

Preparation Time: 10 minutes | Cooking Time: 0 minutes

Servings: 4

Ingredients:

- 1 large, ripe avocado
- 1/4 cup almond milk, sweetened
- 1 tbsp coconut oil
- 1/4 cup cocoa or cacao powder
- 1 tsp vanilla extract

Directions:

1. Process all the fixing using a food processor until smooth and creamy. Chill within 4 hours. Serve and enjoy.

Nutrition:

Calories: 125 kcal; Protein: 1.2 g; Carbs: 6.9 g; Fat: 11.0 g

★ ★ ★ ★ ★

Almond Rice Pudding

Preparation Time: 25 minutes | Cooking Time: 20 minutes

Servings: 6

Ingredients:

- 3 cups almond milk
- 1 cup white rice
- 1/4 cup raw brown sugar
- 1 tsp vanilla
- 1/4 tsp almond extract
- Cinnamon
- 1/4 cup almonds, toasted

Directions:

1. Mix milk plus rice in a medium saucepan. Bring them to a boil. Reduce heat and simmer for 20 minutes with the lid on until the rice is soft.
2. Remove, then put the sugar, vanilla, almond extract, and cinnamon. Put toasted almonds on top, then serve warm.

Nutrition:

Calories: 180 kcal; Fat: 1.5 g; Carbohydrates: 36 g; Protein: 7 g

★ ★ ★ ★ ★

Apples and Cream Shake

Preparation Time: 10 minutes | Cooking Time: 0 minutes

Servings: 4

Ingredients:

- 2 cups vanilla low-fat ice cream
- 1 cup apple sauce
- 1/4 tsp ground cinnamon
- 1 cup fat-free skim milk

Directions:

1. In a blender container, combine the low-fat ice cream, applesauce, and cinnamon. Cover and blend until smooth. Add fat-free skim milk. Cover and blend until mixed. Pour into glasses. Serve immediately.

Nutrition:

Calories: 160 kcal; Fat: 3 g; Carbohydrates: 27 g; Protein: 6 g

★ ★ ★ ★ ★

Measurement Conversion Chart

Volume (Liquid)	Equivalents	
US Standard	**US Standard (oz.)**	**Metric (approximate)**
2 tbsp	1 fl. oz.	30 mL
1/4 cup	2 fl. oz.	60 mL
1/2 cup	4 fl. oz.	120 mL
1 cup	8 fl. oz.	240 mL
1 1/2 cups	12 fl. oz.	355 mL
2 cups or 1 pint	16 fl. oz.	475 mL
4 cups or 1 quart	32 fl. oz.	1 L
gallon	128 fl. oz.	4 L

Volume Equivalents (Dry)

US Standard	Metric (approximate)
1/8 tsp	0.5 mL
1/4 tsp	1 mL
1/2 tsp	2 mL

3/4 tsp	4 mL
1 tsp	5 mL
1 tbsp	15 mL
1/4 cup	59 mL
1/3 cup	79 mL
1/2 cup	118 mL
2/3 cup	156 mL
3/4 cup	177 mL
1 cup	235 mL
2 cups or 1 pint	475 mL
3 cups	700 mL
4 cups or 1 quart	1 L

Oven Temperatures

Fahrenheit (F)	Celsius (C)
250°F	120°C
300°F	150°C
325°F	165°C
50°F	180°C
375°F	190°C
400°F	200°C
425°F	220°C
450°F	230°C

Weight Equivalents

US Standard	Metric
1/2 oz.	1g
1 oz.	3g
2 oz.	6g
4 oz.	11g
8 oz.	22g
12 oz.	34g
16 oz. or 1 lb.	45g

Conclusion

Managing gastroesophageal reflux disease (GERD) by making changes to your diet and lifestyle can effectively reduce symptoms and improve your overall health. By prioritizing foods that are low in acidity, avoiding foods and drinks known to worsen GERD symptoms, eating smaller and more frequent meals, and maintaining a healthy weight, individuals with GERD can experience relief and enhance their quality of life.

This cookbook offers a wide range of delicious and nutritious recipes suitable for those with GERD. From breakfast to dinner, and even snacks and desserts, these recipes are designed to be easy to prepare and enjoyable to eat. They also include a variety of ingredients that are known to be beneficial for GERD, such as ginger, chamomile, and licorice.

Furthermore, this book provides information on lifestyle changes, such as avoiding eating close to bedtime and engaging in regular exercise, that can also help to alleviate GERD symptoms.

It is important to remember that everyone's experience with GERD is unique, and what works for one person may not work for another. It is advisable to seek personalized guidance from a healthcare practitioner or a nutritionist. However, with the right dietary and lifestyle modifications, individuals with GERD can find relief and improve their quality of life.

We are confident that the recipes presented in this cookbook will assist you in improving your health and living a more fulfilling life. Remember, the best gift you can offer your loved ones and the world is a healthy and happy you!